THE PRAISES OF WISDOM

THE PRAISES OF WISDOM

BEING PART I OF

THE BOOK OF WISDOM

A REVISED TRANSLATION
WITH NOTES BY

E. H. BLAKENEY, M.A

*'Wisdom is offered as a blessing in herself.
She is the strength of Life now, the earnest
of what Life is to come.'*
JOHN RUSKIN

OXFORD
BASIL BLACKWELL
1937

Printed and made in Great Britain at
the Shakespeare Head Press
St Aldates Oxford

HOC OPUSCULUM QUALECUNQUE
LIBERIS MEIS DILECTIS
HODIE DEDICO
NON SINE PRECIBUS
UT SAPIENTIAM PERSEQUENTES
CONSEQUANTUR

PREFACE

MY ONE object in setting forth this slender volume is to persuade people to familiarize themselves with one of the finest fragments of Jewish 'wisdom literature.' To this end only the first half of the Book of Wisdom is here printed: it is a self-contained unit, and, in my judgement, all the more impressive when detached from its sequel (chapters x to the end).

An attempt has been made to present this first half in a form suited not only to the ordinary reader but to those also who know enough Greek to follow the original with tolerable ease. The translation is based on the Authorized Version, but a great many new renderings have been incorporated. I hope, though I cannot be sure, that I have managed to preserve something of the stately rhythm of the old rendering, with its moving cadences.

The Introductory note—it does not profess to be more —may perhaps be deemed too brief; but it seemed a work of supererogation to compile a lengthy introduction when readers can so readily have recourse to such works as Oesterley's *The Books of the Apocrypha*, Maldwyn Hughes' *The Ethics of Jewish Apocryphal Literature*, or Fairweather's *The Background of the Gospels*; and there are many more. The notes are plainly not intended for professed scholars; they are of a somewhat elementary character. But within their limits they may perhaps be found adequate for a proper understanding of the text. Greek students may, possibly, find the glossarial Index helpful.

In conclusion I should like to thank the Rev. W. J. Ferrar for kindly examining the proofs of this unpretentious little volume.

Winchester.   E.H.B.

POSTSCRIPT

WHILE these sheets were passing through the press, the newspapers recorded the farewell speech of the Prime Minister, Mr Baldwin, in the House of Commons, on May 5. At the close of one of the paragraphs I found these words: 'The one thing we must pray for in this Country, not only in our Statesmen but in our Leaders of Trades Unions, and in the Masters, is—Wisdom.' Surely they form a fitting pendant to what we read in the great sixth chapter of the *Book of Wisdom*. Never was chapter more profoundly right in teaching and intention, nor one more appropriate to the peculiar circumstances of this, the Coronation year.

CONTENTS

INTRODUCTORY NOTE

THE *Wisdom of Solomon*—such is the Greek title—is one of the Apocryphal books of the Old Testament, and belongs to that class of literature known as Wisdom-literature (the Sapiential books), other examples of which may be seen in Proverbs and Ecclesiastes among canonical scriptures, and in Sirach (Ben Sira, or Ecclesiasticus) and parts of 1 Esdras among the non-canonical. Wisdom literature is not peculiar to Judaism ; it is part of a world-literature. It was international in character, and specimens of it are exhibited in such collections as the Maxims of Ptah-hotep (Egyptian), the teaching of Amen-em-hop (also Egyptian), and in the proverbs of Ahikar, Grand Vizier of Sennacherib.[1] These were all, more or less, traditional books: their object was mainly practical, their teaching based largely on considerations of worldly prudence. But the Hebrew writers have succeeded in importing into their discussions an ethical and religious character.

Of the Hebrew Wisdom-books, our Book of Wisdom, though not mentioned by name in any pre-Christian writer, is the most valuable, in some respects, though we cannot overlook the importance of Job, Proverbs, the later Psalms, and Sirach—the peculiarity of whose doctrine is the identification of the Law with Wisdom. As early as Jeremiah (whose activities extended from 626–586 B.C.) there was a definite order of Wise Men (cf. xviii. 18), distinguishable from Priests and Prophets. What marks the Book of Wisdom is this: though the author writes as an orthodox Jew he was familiar with Greek thought, and expounds a doctrine of immortality more

[1] See Charles, *Apocr. and Pseudepigr.*, vol. ii; Oesterley on Proverbs xxxiv f.

B

clearly than heretofore in Hebrew writings. From the fact that Solomon is often introduced as speaker though never named, the book has received its familiar title 'The Wisdom of Solomon.'[1] The author is employing the king's name as the best method of communicating his own views. The book, then, is a Pseudepigraph. The literary device of attaching a celebrated name to a treatise is common enough: the book of Enoch (or Daniel) is a good example. Such a device may well seem strange nowadays: but in ancient times the compilers of pseudepigraphs were not guilty of any conscious fraud in following a convention.

The object the author had before him in writing the first half of Wisdom is twofold: (1) to combat the Epicurean tendencies[2] of Ecclesiastes; this is noticeable in ii. 1–9, which is a diatribe both against these and certain Sadducean influences that were a feature of the age; (2) to confront the Hellenistic philosophy, taught by Alexandrian Jews, with the glory and majesty of the Law. Faced with the philosophic activities of Alexandria—the focal point of the Diaspora—our author exhibits the Jewish conception of Wisdom (σοφία), making it central to his doctrine, and at the same time endeavouring to bring within the ambit of that doctrine what, in his eyes, might be taken over from Greece and harmonized with Jewish thought as based on the revelation of God in the pages of the Old Testament.

The book, as we have it, may be divided into two portions: chapters i–ix, and x to the end. The first part is, in

---

[1] But the book is frequently cited as, simply, *Wisdom*: see Swete, *Introd. to O.T. in Greek*, p. 267. For an admirable comparison of Wisdom with Ecclesiastes see Dean Plumptre's ed. of the latter work. For the history of the *Apocrypha* in the Church it is enough to refer to the article in Hastings' *D.B.* Cf. too the Sixth Article in our Prayer Book.

[2] In this respect the book may well be compared with the *Axiochus* (of pseudo-Plato), a dialogue which has not only distinct Orphic tendencies but sets forth a doctrine in contrast with the Epicurean.

the proper signification, Wisdom-literature; the second a quasi-philosophy of history, or perhaps rather a homiletical commentary on the early history of Israel. Naturally, it is largely concerned with a polemic against idolatry, especially against idolatry as manifested in Egyptian zoolatry. The author is anxious to contrast the evil results of paganism with the enlightenment vouchsafed to his own countrymen in their sacred scriptures. The suggestion has been made that Part II consists of the Hellenic Passover Haggada; then the original 'Wisdom' and that Passover Haggada fragment were joined together, and so grew to be treated as a single book.

The learned have not yet decided whether Wisdom is of single or dual authorship; but most editors do, in fact, believe in its unity, though it is admittedly hard to acquiesce in this belief.[1] Part I is simple and direct in statement, and often noble in diction; Part II is moody, and, apart from some striking sections, a trifle tiresome and commonplace. In favour of a dual authorship may be adduced the fact that Part I is filled with references to, and high praise of, Wisdom; this is noticeably absent in Part II. If the book is *not* composite, but the result of *one* man's thought, we might infer that it consists of two quite separate treatises, written at widely different dates but brought together into an uneasy cohesion. Have we not some faint resemblance to this in English literature? *The Lover's Tale* (about 1830) was followed, nearly half a century later, by its sequel, *The Golden Supper*. On critical grounds it might not be difficult to show that the two poems were the work of different authors; yet we know that Tennyson was the author of them both.

What is the concept of Wisdom as revealed by the book

[1] For all that can be said in defence of a single authorship, see Oesterley's *The Books of the Apocrypha*, and S. A. Cook, *The Old Testament, a re-interpretation* (1936).

itself? To Jehovah is assigned its source; He and none other is its parent and original (cf. Sirach i. 1–10, Job xxviii. 12–28). The writer of the book identifies Wisdom with the 'holy spirit of the Lord,' and also with the 'Word' in its Jewish meaning. Wisdom is not conceived of as a separate entity, lying outside Godhead, though some texts might seem to suggest this—and perhaps, for artistic purposes, it is so represented in the earlier chapters of Proverbs; rather it is thought of as an all-pervading power, existing within the divine nature; that is, immanent in deity. Despite a certain wavering of view, the writer remains a monotheist, in the strictest sense, throughout. His attitude to Wisdom is closely akin to that of Philo in his approach to the Logos—the logos of Stoicism under a Jewish name. There is one curious omission in the book: nowhere do we find any pronounced Messianic hope. Nor does Isaiah's 'suffering servant' find a counterpart, unless, with Margoliouth, we are to suppose that he is implied in the portrait of the Just Man of chapters i–vi. We find no expectation of any personal Saviour or Redeemer; it is the idea of Israel's destined dominion over the world, and of the universality of Jehovah-worship, that floats before the writer's vision of futurity. There is no doctrine of resurrection; that idea was native to Palestinian theology. But we do find a strong emphasis laid on the manifold love of God, a belief which is avowed with tenderness and beauty of exposition.

The date of the book is wholly uncertain, but it was certainly later than Sirach, earlier than Philo. Enough to say that it was composed 'somewhere in the first century B.C.' The place of origin was Alexandria. No existing work, says Westcott, perhaps more completely represents

---

[1] Cf. Gibson on Job, p. ix; Driver, *Introd to O.T*; Farrar, *Hist. of Interpretation*, 126; Edersheim, *Life and Times of Jesus the Messiah*, i, pp. 31–4; Tyler on Ecclesiastes, sec. 21.

the style of composition that would be produced by the sophistic school of rhetoric as it existed under the conditions of Greek life in that city. Although, writes Dr Edwyn Bevan, the Greek-speaking Jew who wrote it knew the style of Hebrew poetry—perhaps only through the LXX version—he was familiar with the phraseology of the Greek Stoics, and made a kind of blend, which is often impressive, of Greek rhetoric and Hebrew poetical forms. Compare with this the remarks of Mahafty in the twentieth chapter of his very interesting volume *Greek Life and Thought*.

To the oft-discussed question: 'Did the N.T. writers make use of the book?' no definite answer can be given. Paul was probably acquainted with it; still more probably the unknown author of the Hebrews. If Luther's guess be right—and there is no better one—that Hebrews was the work of Apollos, then we might say with some confidence that he *was* acquainted with Wisdom. Was not Apollos an Alexandrian Jew?[1] In the Apostolic Fathers I have failed to discover more than three direct references.

The fact that the book of Wisdom is transitional may perhaps help us to understand why its wisdom-teaching lies half-way between that of the O.T. view of wisdom and the later logos-doctrine.[2] Wisdom is itself the intermediary between God and His works. It was in this way that the book prepared a path for Philo, as Philo for the writer of the fourth Gospel.

[1] See the remarks of H. St John Thackeray in his book, *The Relation of St Paul to Contemporary Jewish Thought*. It is conceivable that the Book of Wisdom may have, to some slight degree, left its traces on the Psalms of the Pharisees (generally known as the *Psalms of Solomon*), but the matter is uncertain, though that there are occasional verbal correspondencies cannot be denied.

[2] See Liddon's *Bampton Lectures*, chap. ii, and Bigg's remarks in his *Christian Platonists of Alexandria*, chap. i.

ANALYSIS

CHAP. I. Rulers and Kings are urged to seek after God and to eschew unrighteousness, which, separating from Him, leads to death. Wisdom is the pre-eminent thing and, coming from God, fills the world. The sinner cannot escape the divine vengeance; lawlessness and apostacy entail destruction, which is brought about through man's own grievous fault, notwithstanding that God desires not the death of any. But the way of Wisdom leads to immortality.

II. The wicked, deeming this life short and grievous, and holding no belief in a Hereafter, resolve to take their pleasures now, regardless of the future. The righteous man they scorn, for his life is a standing reproach to their own. They plot against the afflicted and the aged, because, owing to unbelief, they are blinded with insolence and pride. Regarding not God, who created man for immortality, they strike a pact with Death; wherefore punishment awaits them at the last.

III, IV. After death the righteous have nothing to fear, because, their earthly sorrows ended, they rest with God; whereas vengeance is prepared for the unrighteous and for their children after them. Better, far, a brief and virtuous life than a godless old age. True, a good man may die ere his time, but he is the heir of immortality. Not so with the wicked; their very memory is doomed to perish.

V. Consider the remorse of the wicked, how bitter it will be! Though they confess their sins at the last, this will not avail them; and, when they mark the reward of the godly, great will be their amazement. To those that have ordered their doings aright, honour and glory and divine protection; but God will visit His enemies with the fearful penalty of annihilation.

VI. An appeal to Rulers.—Kings should heed wisdom, for royal power comes from God, to whom all earthly potentates must give account, seeing that He is no respecter of persons.

Moreover, Wisdom is not hard to find; therefore kings should ensue it. Not only is it the secret of power, but it brings with it promotion from on high. A wise ruler is a stay and support to his subjects. Furthermore, a knowledge of Wisdom is freely promised to all that are willing to receive it faithfully.

VII. 'Linea mors rerum.' Even Solomon, notwithstanding all his glory, was born as other folk, and as other folk so will he die. Preferring Wisdom to any other gift, he was granted, in answer to prayer, all the treasures of earthly knowledge. Now the fulness of knowledge comes from God, who is the source of it. The power of the Most High is always and everywhere in operation. The splendour and nature of Wisdom, the possession of which enables men to become friends of God.

VIII. Wisdom's universal dominion. Solomon's love for her, first because Wisdom resembles God, second because the man that has Wisdom possesses all things good. She teaches the virtues, gives intelligence and clearness of judgement, and is therefore of supreme value to rulers. Given Wisdom, the King governed prudently and won renown, both public and private. Aware of her divine origin, Solomon approached God and so prayed that the guerdon of Wisdom might be his.

IX and XI, 23–end. 'I am weak; hence I need Wisdom at my side to guide me aright in the duties of kingship. Without her, even the mighty are but as dust in the balance. Man is ignorant; his soul is cumbered with a body; he cannot hope to attain to heavenly things unless Wisdom is at hand to counsel him.'
Finally God, although so great and majestic in operation, rules not only by power, but still more through His mercy and His love.

ΣΟΦΙΑ ΣΑΛΩΜΩΝΟΣ

1

Ἀγαπήσατε δικαιοσύνην οἱ κρίνοντες τὴν γῆν, φρονή-
σατε περὶ τοῦ Κυρίου ἐν ἀγαθότητι, καὶ ἐν ἁπλότητι
2 καρδίας ζητήσατε αὐτόν. Ὅτι εὑρίσκεται τοῖς μὴ πειρά-
ζουσιν αὐτόν, ἐμφανίζεται δὲ τοῖς μὴ ἀπιστοῦσιν αὐτῷ.
3 Σκολιοὶ γὰρ λογισμοὶ χωρίζουσιν ἀπὸ Θεοῦ, δοκιμα-
ζομένη τε ἡ δύναμις ἐλέγχει τοὺς ἄφρονας.
4 Ὅτι εἰς κακότεχνον ψυχὴν οὐκ εἰσελεύσεται σοφία,
5 οὐδὲ κατοικήσει ἐν σώματι κατάχρεῳ ἁμαρτίας. Ἅγιον
γὰρ πνεῦμα παιδείας φεύξεται δόλον, καὶ ἀπαναστήσεται
ἀπὸ λογισμῶν ἀσυνέτων, καὶ ἐλεγχθήσεται ἐπελθούσης
6 ἀδικίας. Φιλάνθρωπον γὰρ πνεῦμα σοφία, καὶ οὐκ ἀθωώσει
βλάσφημον ἀπὸ χειλέων αὐτοῦ, ὅτι τῶν νεφρῶν αὐτοῦ
μάρτυς ὁ Θεός, καὶ τῆς καρδίας αὐτοῦ ἐπίσκοπος ἀληθής,
7 καὶ τῆς γλώσσης ἀκουστής. Ὅτι πνεῦμα Κυρίου πεπλή-
ρωκε τὴν οἰκουμένην, καὶ τὸ συνέχον τὰ πάντα γνῶσιν
ἔχει φωνῆς.
8 Διὰ τοῦτο φθεγγόμενος ἄδικα οὐδεὶς μὴ λάθῃ, οὐδὲ μὴν
9 παροδεύσῃ αὐτὸν ἐλέγχουσα ἡ δίκη. Ἐν γὰρ διαβουλίοις
ἀσεβοῦς ἐξέτασις ἔσται, λόγων δὲ αὐτοῦ ἀκοὴ πρὸς Κύριον
10 ἥξει εἰς ἔλεγχον ἀνομημάτων αὐτοῦ. Ὅτι οὖς ζηλώσεως
ἀκροᾶται τὰ πάντα, καὶ θροῦς γογγυσμῶν οὐκ ἀπο-
κρύπτεται.
11 Φυλάξασθε τοίνυν γογγυσμὸν ἀνωφελῆ, καὶ ἀπὸ κατα-
λαλιᾶς φείσασθε γλώσσης· ὅτι φθέγμα λαθραῖον κενὸν
οὐ πορεύσεται, στόμα δὲ καταψευδόμενον ἀναιρεῖ ψυχήν.
12 Μὴ ζηλοῦτε θάνατον ἐν πλάνῃ ζωῆς ὑμῶν, μηδὲ ἐπι-
13 σπᾶσθε ὄλεθρον ἔργοις χειρῶν ὑμῶν, ὅτι ὁ Θεὸς θάνατον

THE PRAISES OF WISDOM

Chapter I

LOVE righteousness, ye that judge the earth; let your thoughts concerning the Lord be in uprightness, and in simplicity of heart seek Him; because He is found of them that tempt Him not, and manifesteth Himself unto such as trust Him.

For perverse dealings separate from God, and His power, when put to the test, bringeth the unwise to shame.

Into an evil-devising soul Wisdom entereth not, nor maketh its habitation in a body forfeit unto sin. For a holy spirit of discipline will shun deceit, and will remove from foolish reasonings, and will be put to shame when unrighteousness hath entered in. For Wisdom is a spirit that loveth mankind, and so will not acquit a blasphemer of his words, because God is witness of his reins, and a true overseer of his heart and a hearer of his tongue. For the spirit of the Lord hath filled the world, and that which holdeth the Universe together hath knowledge of the voice.

Wherefore no man that speaketh unrighteous words shall be hid, nor indeed shall justice, when it convicteth, pass him by. Surely into the counsels of the ungodly shall inquisition be made, and the sound of his words shall come before the Lord, to the punishment of his lawless deeds. For an Ear of jealousy heareth all things, and a noise of murmurings is not concealed.

Guard then against murmuring, which profiteth not, and refrain thy lips from speaking against God; for there is no word so secret that it shall go void, and a lying mouth slayeth the soul.

Seek not after death in the error of your life, neither pull destruction on yourselves with the works of your own hands.

14 οὐκ ἐποίησεν, οὐδὲ τέρπεται ἐπ' ἀπωλείᾳ ζώντων. Ἔκτισε γὰρ εἰς τὸ εἶναι τὰ πάντα, καὶ σωτήριοι αἱ γενέσεις τοῦ κόσμου, καὶ οὐκ ἔστιν ἐν αὐταῖς φάρμακον ὀλέθρου, οὔτε 15 ᾅδου βασίλειον ἐπὶ γῆς. Δικαιοσύνη γὰρ ἀθάνατός ἐστιν· 16 ἀσεβεῖς δὲ ταῖς χερσὶ καὶ τοῖς λόγοις προσεκαλέσαντο αὐτὸν, φίλον ἡγησάμενοι αὐτὸν ἐτάκησαν, καὶ συνθήκην ἔθεντο πρὸς αὐτὸν, ὅτι ἄξιοί εἰσι τῆς ἐκείνου μερίδος εἶναι.

2

Εἶπον γὰρ ἑαυτοῖς λογισάμενοι οὐκ ὀρθῶς, Ὀλίγος ἐστὶ καὶ λυπηρὸς ὁ βίος ἡμῶν καὶ οὐκ ἔστιν ἴασις ἐν τελευτῇ 2 ἀνθρώπου, καὶ οὐκ ἐγνώσθη ὁ ἀναλύσας ἐξ ᾅδου. Ὅτι αὐτοσχεδίως ἐγεννήθημεν, καὶ μετὰ τοῦτο ἐσόμεθα ὡς οὐχ ὑπάρξαντες, ὅτι καπνὸς ἡ πνοὴ ἐν ῥισὶν ἡμῶν, καὶ ὁ λόγος 3 σπινθὴρ ἐν κινήσει καρδίας ἡμῶν, οὗ σβεσθέντος τέφρα ἀποβήσεται τὸ σῶμα, καὶ τὸ πνεῦμα διαχυθήσεται ὡς 4 χαῦνος ἀήρ· καὶ τὸ ὄνομα ἡμῶν ἐπιλησθήσεται ἐν χρόνῳ, καὶ οὐθεὶς μνημονεύσει τῶν ἔργων ἡμῶν, καὶ παρελεύσεται ὁ βίος ἡμῶν ὡς ἴχνη νεφέλης, καὶ ὡς ὁμίχλη διασκεδασθήσεται διωχθεῖσα ὑπὸ ἀκτίνων ἡλίου καὶ ὑπὸ θερμότητος αὐτοῦ βαρυνθεῖσα.

5 Σκιᾶς γὰρ πάροδος ὁ βίος ἡμῶν, καὶ οὐκ ἔστιν ἀναποδισμὸς τῆς τελευτῆς ἡμῶν, ὅτι κατεσφραγίσθη, καὶ οὐδεὶς 6 ἀναστρέφει. Δεῦτε οὖν καὶ ἀπολαύσωμεν τῶν ὄντων ἀγαθῶν, καὶ χρησώμεθα τῇ κτίσει ὡς νεότητι σπουδαίως. 7 Οἴνου πολυτελοῦς καὶ μύρων πλησθῶμεν, καὶ μὴ παροδευ- 8 σάτω ἡμᾶς ἄνθος ἀέρος. Στεψώμεθα ῥόδων κάλυξι πρὶν ἢ 9 μαρανθῆναι. Μηδεὶς ἡμῶν ἄμοιρος ἔστω τῆς ἡμετέρας ἀγερωχίας, πανταχῇ καταλίπωμεν σύμβολα τῆς εὐφροσύνης, ὅτι αὕτη ἡ μερὶς ἡμῶν καὶ ὁ κλῆρος οὗτος.

For God made not death, neither hath He pleasure in the ruin of the living. He formed all things that they might have their true being, and the creatures of nature are healthful in their generations; neither is there any poison of destruction in them, nor hath Death a realm on earth. For righteousness is immortal [but the gain of unrighteousness is death]. Nevertheless the ungodly with their works and words summoned Death, and, because they cherished Death, they melted away and made with Death a covenant inasmuch as they are worthy of his lot.

CHAPTER II

FOR the ungodly said within themselves, reasoning perversely: 'Our life is brief and full of sorrow, and at the hour of death there is no remedy, neither was any man known to have returned from the grave. For we were born at all adventure, and hereafter we shall be as though we had never been, because the breath in our nostrils is as smoke, and reason but a spark in the beating of our heart; which being put out the body will turn to ashes and the spirit dissolve as thin air, and our name will be forgotten in time and no man have our works in remembrance; and life shall fade as the footsteps of a cloud, scattered as a mist when driven by the rays of the sun and smitten by the heat thereof.

'For our span is the passing of a shadow, and there is no putting back of our end; it is fast sealed, and none returneth. Come, therefore, let us delight in our good things, and zealously enjoy the world in the days of our youth. Let us fill ourselves with costly wines and [anoint us] with unguents, nor let any spring flower pass us by. Let us crown ourselves with rose-buds or ever they be withered; let there be no meadow untraversed by our revels; let us leave tokens of our jollity in every place; for this is our portion, and our lot is this.

10 Καταδυναστεύσωμεν πένητα δίκαιον, μὴ φεισώμεθα
χήρας, μηδὲ πρεσβύτου ἐντραπῶμεν πολιὰς πολυχρονίους.
11 Ἔστω δὲ ἡμῶν ἡ ἰσχὺς νόμος τῆς δικαιοσύνης, τὸ γὰρ
12 ἀσθενὲς ἄχρηστον ἐλέγχεται. Ἐνεδρεύσωμεν δὲ τὸν δίκαιον,
ὅτι δύσχρηστος ἡμῖν ἐστι, καὶ ἐναντιοῦται τοῖς ἔργοις
ἡμῶν, καὶ ὀνειδίζει ἡμῖν ἁμαρτήματα νόμου, καὶ ἐπιφημίζει
13 ἡμῖν ἁμαρτήματα παιδείας ἡμῶν· ἐπαγγέλλεται γνῶσιν
14 ἔχειν Θεοῦ, καὶ παῖδα Κυρίου ἑαυτὸν ὀνομάζει. Ἐγένετο
15 ἡμῖν εἰς ἔλεγχον ἐννοιῶν ἡμῶν. Βαρύς ἐστιν ἡμῖν καὶ
βλεπόμενος, ὅτι ἀνόμοιος τοῖς ἄλλοις ὁ βίος αὐτοῦ, καὶ
ἐξηλλαγμέναι αἱ τρίβοι αὐτοῦ.
16 Εἰς κίβδηλον ἐλογίσθημεν αὐτῷ, καὶ ἀπέχεται τῶν ὁδῶν
ἡμῶν ὡς ἀπὸ ἀκαθαρσιῶν· μακαρίζει ἔσχατα δικαίων, καὶ
ἀλαζονεύεται πατέρα Θεόν.
17 Ἴδωμεν εἰ οἱ λόγοι αὐτοῦ ἀληθεῖς, καὶ πειράσωμεν τὰ ἐν
18 ἐκβάσει αὐτοῦ. Εἰ γάρ ἐστιν ὁ δίκαιος υἱὸς Θεοῦ, ἀντιλή-
ψεται αὐτοῦ, καὶ ῥύσεται αὐτὸν ἐκ χειρὸς ἀνθεστηκότων.
19 Ὕβρει καὶ βασάνῳ ἐτάσωμεν αὐτόν, ἵνα γνῶμεν τὴν ἐπιεί-
κειαν αὐτοῦ, καὶ δοκιμάσωμεν τὴν ἀνεξικακίαν αὐτοῦ.
20 Θανάτῳ ἀσχήμονι καταδικάσωμεν αὐτόν, ἔσται γὰρ
αὐτοῦ ἐπισκοπὴ ἐκ λόγων αὐτοῦ.
21,22 Ταῦτα ἐλογίσαντο, καὶ ἐπλανήθησαν· ἀπετύφλωσε γὰρ
αὐτοὺς ἡ κακία αὐτῶν, καὶ οὐκ ἔγνωσαν μυστήρια Θεοῦ,
οὐδὲ μισθὸν ἤλπισαν ὁσιότητος, οὐδὲ ἔκριναν γέρας ψυχῶν
23 ἀμώμων. Ὅτι ὁ Θεὸς ἔκτισε τὸν ἄνθρωπον ἐπ᾽ ἀφθαρσίᾳ,
24 καὶ εἰκόνα τῆς ἰδίας ἀϊδιότητος ἐποίησεν αὐτόν. Φθόνῳ δὲ
διαβόλου θάνατος εἰσῆλθεν εἰς τὸν κόσμον, πειράζουσι δὲ
αὐτὸν οἱ τῆς ἐκείνου μερίδος ὄντες.

'Let us crush the poor righteous man, nor spare the widow, neither reverence the grey hairs of the aged. Let our strength be unto us a law of justice, for that which is feeble is accounted of no price. Let us set a snare for the righteous man, for he is unserviceable to us and clean contrary to our doings; he upraideth us for transgressing the Law, and reproacheth us with trespass against our discipline. He boasteth that he hath knowledge of God, and calleth himself a son of the Lord. He became unto us a reproof of our imaginations; he is grievous even to behold, because his life is not as other men's; his ways are changed.

'We were esteemed of him as dross, and he abstaineth from our fashion as from filth; he deemeth the end of the just to be blessed, and vaunteth himself that God is his father.

'Let us see if his words be true, and prove what shall befall him at his death. For if the righteous man is a son of God, God will uphold him and deliver him out of the hand of his enemies. With insult and with torment let us test him, that we may know his meekness and prove his forbearance. To a shameful death let us condemn him, for, according to his own words, God will visit him.'

So they reasoned, and went astray, for malice blinded them. As for the mysteries of God, they knew them not, neither hoped they for the recompense of holiness nor judged that there is a reward for the innocent. For God created man to be immortal, and made him to be an image of His own eternity; howbeit, through envy of the Devil, death entered into the world, and they that be of his part have experience thereof.

3

Δικαίων δὲ ψυχαὶ ἐν χειρὶ Θεοῦ, καὶ οὐ μὴ ἅψηται αὐτῶν
2 βάσανος. Ἔδοξαν ἐν ὀφθαλμοῖς ἀφρόνων τεθνάναι, καὶ ἐλο-
3 γίσθη κάκωσις ἡ ἔξοδος αὐτῶν, καὶ ἡ ἀφ' ἡμῶν πορεία
4 σύντριμμα· οἱ δέ εἰσιν ἐν εἰρήνῃ. Καὶ γὰρ ἐν ὄψει ἀνθρώπων
5 ἐὰν κολασθῶσιν, ἡ ἐλπὶς αὐτῶν ἀθανασίας πλήρης. Καὶ
ὀλίγα παιδευθέντες μεγάλα εὐεργετηθήσονται, ὅτι ὁ Θεὸς
6 ἐπείρασεν αὐτούς, καὶ εὗρεν αὐτοὺς ἀξίους ἑαυτοῦ. Ὡς
χρυσὸν ἐν χωνευτηρίῳ ἐδοκίμασεν αὐτούς, καὶ ὡς ὁλοκάρ-
7 πωμα θυσίας προσεδέξατο αὐτούς. Καὶ ἐν καιρῷ ἐπισκοπῆς
αὐτῶν ἀναλάμψουσι, καὶ ὡς σπινθῆρες ἐν καλάμῃ διαδρα-
8 μοῦνται. Κρινοῦσιν ἔθνη καὶ κρατήσουσι λαῶν, καὶ βασι-
9 λεύσει αὐτῶν Κύριος εἰς τοὺς αἰῶνας. Οἱ πεποιθότες ἐπ'
αὐτῷ συνήσουσιν ἀλήθειαν, καὶ οἱ πιστοὶ ἐν ἀγάπῃ
προσμενοῦσιν αὐτῷ, ὅτι χάρις καὶ ἔλεος τοῖς ἐκλεκτοῖς
10 αὐτοῦ. Οἱ δὲ ἀσεβεῖς καθὰ ἐλογίσαντο ἕξουσιν ἐπιτιμίαν,
οἱ ἀμελήσαντες τοῦ δικαίου καὶ τοῦ Κυρίου ἀποστάντες.
11 Σοφίαν γὰρ καὶ παιδείαν ὁ ἐξουθενῶν ταλαίπωρος, καὶ
κενὴ ἡ ἐλπὶς αὐτῶν, καὶ οἱ κόποι ἀνόνητοι, καὶ ἄχρηστα
12 τὰ ἔργα αὐτῶν. Αἱ γυναῖκες αὐτῶν ἄφρονες, καὶ πονηρὰ
13 τὰ τέκνα αὐτῶν· ἐπικατάρατος ἡ γένεσις αὐτῶν. ὅτι
μακαρία στεῖρα ἡ ἀμίαντος, ἥτις οὐκ ἔγνω κοίτην ἐν παρα-
14 πτώματι· ἕξει καρπὸν ἐν ἐπισκοπῇ ψυχῶν. Καὶ εὐνοῦχος
ὁ μὴ ἐργασάμενος ἐν χειρὶ ἀνόμημα, μηδὲ ἐνθυμηθεὶς κατὰ
τοῦ Κυρίου πονηρά, δοθήσεται γὰρ αὐτῷ τῆς πίστεως
χάρις ἐκλεκτή, καὶ κλῆρος ἐν ναῷ Κυρίου θυμηρέστερος.
15 Ἀγαθῶν γὰρ πόνων καρπὸς εὐκλεής, καὶ ἀδιάπτωτος ἡ
ῥίζα τῆς φρονήσεως.

CHAPTER III

BUT the souls of the righteous are in the hand of God, and there shall no torment touch them. In the judgement of fools they seemed to be dead and their going hence was taken for misfortune and their departure from us to be annihilation; nevertheless they are in peace. For even though in the sight of men they be punished, yet is their hope full of immortality; and having been chastened a little, great shall be their recompense, because God hath tested them and proved them worthy of Himself. As gold in a refiner's furnace, so He tried them, and as a whole burnt-offering He accepted them. In the time of their visitation they shall shine forth, and run to and fro like sparks in stubble. They shall judge nations and rule over peoples, and the Lord shall be their King for evermore. They that put their trust in Him will understand truth, and such as be faithful will abide with Him in love; for grace and mercy belong unto His chosen. But the ungodly shall be punished according to their own devices, even they that have lightly esteemed the righteous man and forsaken the Lord.

They that despise wisdom and discipline are wretched; their faith is vain, their labour profitless, their works ineffectual. Their wives are foolish and their children evil. Cursed is their birth, because blessed is the barren woman that is undefiled, who hath not conceived in sin; she shall bear fruit in the visitation of souls. Blessed withal is the eunuch that hath wrought no iniquity nor devised evil against the Lord; for unto him will be given a chosen grace of faith, and a portion in the Lord's sanctuary more desirable. For glorious is the fruit of good labours, and the root of understanding faileth not.

16 Τέκνα δὲ μοιχῶν ἀτέλεστα ἔσται, καὶ ἐκ παρανόμου
17 κοίτης σπέρμα ἀφανισθήσεται. Ἐάν τε γὰρ μακρόβιοι
γένωνται, εἰς οὐθὲν λογισθήσονται, καὶ ἄτιμον ἐπ' ἐσχάτων
18 τὸ γῆρας αὐτῶν. Ἐάν τε ὀξέως τελευτήσωσιν, οὐχ ἕξουσιν
19 ἐλπίδα, οὐδὲ ἐν ἡμέρᾳ διαγνώσεως παραμύθιον. Γενεᾶς
γὰρ ἀδίκου χαλεπὰ τὰ τέλη.

4

Κρείσσων ἀτεκνία μετὰ ἀρετῆς, ἀθανασία γάρ ἐστιν ἐν
μνήμῃ αὐτῆς, ὅτι καὶ παρὰ Θεῷ γινώσκεται καὶ παρὰ
2 ἀνθρώποις. Παροῦσάν τε μιμοῦνται αὐτὴν, καὶ ποθοῦσιν
ἀπελθοῦσαν, καὶ ἐν τῷ αἰῶνι στεφανηφοροῦσα πομπεύει
τὸν τῶν ἀμιάντων ἄθλων ἀγῶνα νικήσασα.
3 Πολύγονον δὲ ἀσεβῶν πλῆθος οὐ χρησιμεύσει, καὶ ἐκ
νόθων μοσχευμάτων οὐ δώσει ῥίζαν εἰς βάθος, οὐδὲ ἀσφαλῆ
4 βάσιν ἑδράσει. Κἂν γὰρ ἐν κλάδοις πρὸς καιρὸν ἀναθάλῃ,
ἐπισφαλῶς βεβηκότα ὑπὸ ἀνέμου σαλευθήσεται, καὶ ὑπὸ
5 βίας ἀνέμων ἐκριζωθήσεται. Περικλασθήσονται κλῶνες
ἀτέλεστοι, καὶ ὁ καρπὸς αὐτῶν ἄχρηστος, ἄωρος εἰς βρῶ-
6 σιν καὶ εἰς οὐθὲν ἐπιτήδειος. Ἐκ γὰρ ἀνόμων ὕπνων τέκνα
γεννώμενα μάρτυρές εἰσι πονηρίας κατὰ γονέων ἐν ἐξετα-
7 σμῷ αὐτῶν. Δίκαιος δὲ ἐὰν φθάσῃ τελευτῆσαι, ἐν ἀνα-
παύσει ἔσται.
8 Γῆρας γὰρ τίμιον οὐ τὸ πολυχρόνιον, οὐδὲ ἀριθμῷ ἐτῶν
9 μεμέτρηται. Πολιὰ δέ ἐστιν φρόνησις ἀνθρώποις, καὶ ἡλικία
γήρως βίος ἀκηλίδωτος.
10 Εὐάρεστος τῷ Θεῷ γενόμενος ἠγαπήθη, καὶ ζῶν μεταξὺ
11 ἁμαρτωλῶν μετετέθη. Ἡρπάγη μὴ κακία ἀλλάξῃ σύνεσιν
12 αὐτοῦ, ἢ δόλος ἀπατήσῃ ψυχὴν αὐτοῦ. Βασκανία γὰρ
φαυλότητος ἀμαυροῖ τὰ καλά, καὶ ῥεμβασμὸς ἐπιθυμίας

But children of adulterers shall not come to ripeness, and the seed of an unlawful bed shall vanish utterly. For though they live long, they will be reckoned for naught, and their end will be dishonoured at the last. And though they die speedily, they shall have no hope, nor comfort in the day of decision. For the evils of an unrighteous generation are grievous.

CHAPTER IV

BETTER childlessness if joined with virtue, for in the remembrance of virtue dwelleth immortality, because it is approved before God and man. When it is present, men take example thereat; when it is gone, they desire it, for it weareth a crown for ever and walketh in triumph, having won victory in the contest for reward undefiled.

But a multiplying host of the godless will not prosper, and from bastard slips they will find no deep root, nor fix a sure foundation. For albeit the branches flourish awhile, yet, biding unsure, they will be shaken by the wind, and by violence of tempests will they be uprooted. Their branches will be broken or ever they come to maturity; their fruit is profitless, unripe as food and of no value. For children begotten of lawless slumbers are witnesses of iniquity against parents, in the day when God maketh inquisition. But a righteous man, though he die untimely, shall be at rest.

An honoured old age standeth not in length of days, neither is measured by the number of its years. But Wisdom is hoary hairs unto men, and unblemished life is a good old age.

Well-pleasing unto God, the righteous man was loved by Him, and, while living among transgressors, he was translated. He was snatched away, lest evil should change his understanding or craft beguile his soul. For the witchery of in-

C

13 μεταλλεύει νοῦν ἄκακον. Τελειωθεὶς ἐν ὀλίγῳ ἐπλήρωσε
14 χρόνους μακρούς, ἀρεστὴ γὰρ ἦν Κυρίῳ ἡ ψυχὴ αὐτοῦ·
διὰ τοῦτο ἔσπευσεν ἐκ μέσου πονηρίας· οἱ δὲ λαοὶ ἰδόντες
15 καὶ μὴ νοήσαντες, μηδὲ θέντες ἐπὶ διανοίᾳ τὸ τοιοῦτο, ὅτι
χάρις καὶ ἔλεος ἐν τοῖς ἐκλεκτοῖς αὐτοῦ, καὶ ἐπισκοπὴ ἐν
τοῖς ὁσίοις αὐτοῦ.
16 Κατακρινεῖ δὲ δίκαιος καμὼν τοὺς ζῶντας ἀσεβεῖς, καὶ
17 νεότης τελεσθεῖσα ταχέως πολυετὲς γῆρας ἀδίκου. Ὄψον-
ται γὰρ τελευτὴν σοφοῦ, καὶ οὐ νοήσουσι τί ἐβουλεύσατο
18 περὶ αὐτοῦ, καὶ εἰς τί ἠσφαλίσατο αὐτὸν ὁ Κύριος· ὄψον-
ται καὶ ἐξουθενήσουσιν, αὐτοὺς δὲ ὁ Κύριος ἐκγελάσεται·
καὶ ἔσονται μετὰ τοῦτο εἰς πτῶμα ἄτιμον, καὶ εἰς ὕβριν ἐν
19 νεκροῖς δι᾽ αἰῶνος, ὅτι ῥήξει αὐτοὺς ἀφώνους πρηνεῖς, καὶ
σαλεύσει αὐτοὺς ἐκ θεμελίων· καὶ ἕως ἐσχάτου χερσωθή-
σονται, καὶ ἔσονται ἐν ὀδύνῃ, καὶ ἡ μνήμη αὐτῶν ἀπο-
20 λεῖται· ἐλεύσονται ἐν συλλογισμῷ ἁμαρτημάτων αὐτῶν
δειλοί, καὶ ἐλέγξει αὐτοὺς ἐξεναντίας τὰ ἀνομήματα αὐτῶν.

5

2 Τότε στήσεται ἐν παρρησίᾳ πολλῇ ὁ δίκαιος κατὰ πρό-
3 σωπον τῶν θλιψάντων αὐτόν, καὶ τῶν ἀθετούντων τοὺς
πόνους αὐτοῦ. Ἰδόντες ταραχθήσονται φόβῳ δεινῷ, καὶ
ἐκστήσονται ἐπὶ τῷ παραδόξῳ τῆς σωτηρίας. Ἐροῦσιν
4 ἑαυτοῖς μετανοοῦντες, καὶ διὰ στενοχωρίαν πνεύματος
5 στενάζοντες, Οὗτος ἦν, ὃν ἔσχομέν ποτε εἰς γέλωτα καὶ εἰς
παραβολὴν ὀνειδισμοῦ· οἱ ἄφρονες τὸν βίον αὐτοῦ ἐλογι-
6 σάμεθα μανίαν, καὶ τὴν τελευτὴν αὐτοῦ ἄτιμον. Πῶς κατε-
λογίσθη ἐν υἱοῖς Θεοῦ καὶ ἐν ἁγίοις ὁ κλῆρος αὐτοῦ ἐστιν;
ἄρα ἐπλανήθημεν ἀπὸ ὁδοῦ ἀληθείας, καὶ τὸ τῆς δικαιοσύνης φῶς οὐκ ἔλαμψεν ἡμῖν, καὶ ὁ ἥλιος οὐκ ἀνέτειλεν ἡμῖν.

iquity darkeneth things that be fair, and the whirl of desire perverteth a guileless heart. Perfected in a brief season, he fulfilled long years. His soul pleased the Lord, therefore He hastened him away from the midst of wickedness. The peoples beheld but comprehended it not, neither laid they to heart such a thing as this, namely, that grace and mercy are with His elect, and His visitation is with His saints.

Thus the righteous that be dead shall condemn the godless that be alive; and youth soon perfected shall condemn the lengthened years of the unrighteous. For they shall see the end of the wise man, and understand what God hath determined concerning him, and wherefore He hath established him in safety. They will look upon him, and despise him; but God shall have them in derision, and hereafter shall they be a corpse dishonoured and a reproach among the dead for evermore. God will rend them asunder; He will strike them down, speechless, and shake them from their foundations. They shall be destroyed utterly, and be in anguish; their memorial shall perish with them. They shall come, in terror, at the reckoning of their iniquities, and their lawless deeds convict them to their face.

CHAPTER V

THEN shall the righteous man stand forth with great confidence, in the presence of them that oppressed him and made light of his labours. At the sight thereof they will be dismayed with grievous fear and be astonished at the wonder of his deliverance. Repenting, and groaning for vexation of spirit, they will say to one another: 'Lo, this was he whom aforetime we mocked and accounted a by-word of reproach; we fools deemed his life madness and his end dishonoured. How came it that he was reckoned among the sons of God, and how is his portion among the saints? Surely we wandered from the path of truth, and the light of righteousness shone not for us, neither did the sun arise upon us. We satisfied ourselves with the ways of lawlessness and destruction; we travelled through

7 Ἀνομίας ἐνεπλήσθημεν τρίβοις καὶ ἀπωλείας, καὶ διωδεύ-
σαμεν ἐρήμους ἀβάτους, τὴν δὲ ὁδὸν Κυρίου οὐκ ἔγνωμεν.

8 Τί ὠφέλησεν ἡμᾶς ἡ ὑπερηφανία; καὶ τί πλοῦτος μετὰ
9 ἀλαζονείας συμβέβληται ἡμῖν; παρῆλθεν ἐκεῖνα πάντα ὡς
10 σκιὰ καὶ ὡς ἀγγελία παρατρέχουσα· ὡς ναῦς διερχομένη
κυμαινόμενον ὕδωρ, ἧς διαβάσης οὐκ ἔστιν ἴχνος εὑρεῖν,
11 οὐδὲ ἀτραπὸν τρόπιος αὐτῆς ἐν κύμασιν· ἢ ὡς ὀρνέου
διϊπτάντος ἀέρα οὐθὲν εὑρίσκεται τεκμήριον πορείας,
πληγῇ δὲ ταρσῶν μαστιζόμενον πνεῦμα κοῦφον καὶ σχιζό-
μενον βίᾳ ῥοίζου, κινουμένων πτερύγων διωδεύθη, καὶ
12 μετὰ τοῦτο οὐχ εὑρέθη σημεῖον ἐπιβάσεως ἐν αὐτῷ· ἢ ὡς
βέλους βληθέντος ἐπὶ σκοπόν, τμηθεὶς ὁ ἀὴρ εὐθέως εἰς
13 ἑαυτὸν ἀνελύθη, ὡς ἀγνοῆσαι τὴν δίοδον αὐτοῦ· οὕτως
καὶ ἡμεῖς γεννηθέντες ἐξελίπομεν· καὶ ἀρετῆς μὲν σημεῖον
οὐδὲν ἔσχομεν δεῖξαι, ἐν δὲ τῇ κακίᾳ ἡμῶν κατεδαπανήθη-
μεν.

14 Ὅτι ἐλπὶς ἀσεβοῦς ὡς φερόμενος χοῦς ὑπὸ ἀνέμου, καὶ
ὡς πάχνη ὑπὸ λαίλαπος διωχθεῖσα λεπτή, καὶ ὡς καπνὸς
ὑπὸ ἀνέμου διεχύθη, καὶ ὡς μνεία καταλύτου μονοημέρου
παρώδευσε.

15 Δίκαιοι δὲ εἰς τὸν αἰῶνα ζῶσι, καὶ ἐν Κυρίῳ ὁ μισθὸς
16 αὐτῶν, καὶ ἡ φροντὶς αὐτῶν παρὰ Ὑψίστῳ. Διὰ τοῦτο
λήψονται τὸ βασίλειον τῆς εὐπρεπείας καὶ τὸ διάδημα τοῦ
κάλλους ἐκ χειρὸς Κυρίου, ὅτι τῇ δεξιᾷ σκεπάσει αὐτούς,
17 καὶ τῷ βραχίονι ὑπερασπιεῖ αὐτῶν. Λήψεται πανοπλίαν
τὸν ζῆλον αὐτοῦ, καὶ ὁπλοποιήσει τὴν κτίσιν εἰς ἄμυναν
18 ἐχθρῶν. Ἐνδύσεται θώρακα δικαιοσύνην, καὶ περιθήσεται
19 κόρυθα κρίσιν ἀνυπόκριτον. Λήψεται ἀσπίδα ἀκατα-
20 μάχητον ὁσιότητα, ὀξυνεῖ δὲ ἀπότομον ὀργὴν εἰς ῥομφαίαν,
συνεκπολεμήσει δὲ αὐτῷ ὁ κόσμος ἐπὶ τοὺς παράφρονας.

deserts where no track lay, but the highway of the Lord we heeded not.

'What profit was there in our pride? What good thing have our wealth and vain-glory bestowed upon us? All those things are passed like a shadow, and as a rumour that speedeth by; as a ship cleaving the troubled deep, whereof, when it hath gone, no trace can be found, neither the pathway of its keel in the waters; or as, when a bird flieth through the air, no token of her passage is found, but the light air, beaten by the stroke of her wings and rent in twain by the strong motion of her pinions, is passed through and afterward no sign of her going is discovered; or as, when an arrow is shot at a mark, the air disparteth and straightway returneth again: even so we, as soon as we were born, ceased to be. Of virtue we bequeathed no token, but in our iniquity were we consumed.'

For the hope of the godless is like chaff carried by the wind, as slender foam driven by the tempest; it is scattered even as a vapour by the storm-wind, and passeth as the remembrance of a guest that tarrieth but for a day.

But the righteous live for evermore; in the Lord is their recompense, and the care of them with the Most High. Therefore shall they receive a kingdom of glory, and a diadem of beauty from the Lord's hand; with His right hand shall He cover them and with His arm shall He shield them. For panoply shall He take His jealousy, and make Creation His weapon to repel His adversaries. He shall don judgement unfeigned as a morion; He shall take holiness as an invincible buckler, but whet His wrath inexorable as a sword; and the Universe shall march with Him to fight against the senseless. There shall go forth thunderbolts, aimed true; and from the clouds,

21 Πορεύσονται εὔστοχοι βολίδες ἀστραπῶν, καὶ ὡς ἀπὸ
22 εὐκύκλου τόξου τῶν νεφῶν ἐπὶ σκοπὸν ἁλοῦνται. Καὶ ἐκ
πετροβόλου θυμοῦ πλήρεις ῥιφήσονται χάλαζαι· ἀγαν-
ακτήσει κατ᾽ αὐτῶν ὕδωρ θαλάσσης, ποταμοὶ δὲ συγκλύ-
23 σουσιν ἀποτόμως. Ἀντιστήσεται αὐτοῖς πνεῦμα δυνάμεως, καὶ ὡς λαίλαψ ἐκλικμήσει αὐτούς· καὶ ἐρημώσει
πᾶσαν τὴν γῆν ἀνομία, καὶ ἡ κακοπραγία περιτρέψει
θρόνους δυναστῶν.

6

Ἀκούσατε οὖν, βασιλεῖς, καὶ σύνετε· μάθετε, δικασταὶ
2 περάτων γῆς. Ἐνωτίσασθε, οἱ κρατοῦντες πλήθους καὶ
3 γεγαυρωμένοι ἐπὶ ὄχλοις ἐθνῶν. Ὅτι ἐδόθη παρὰ τοῦ
Κυρίου ἡ κράτησις ὑμῖν, καὶ ἡ δυναστεία παρὰ Ὑψίστου,
ὃς ἐξετάσει ὑμῶν τὰ ἔργα, καὶ τὰς βουλὰς διερευνήσει.
4 Ὅτι ὑπηρέται ὄντες τῆς αὐτοῦ βασιλείας οὐκ ἐκρίνατε
ὀρθῶς, οὐδὲ ἐφυλάξατε νόμον, οὐδὲ κατὰ τὴν βουλὴν τοῦ
5 Θεοῦ ἐπορεύθητε, φρικτῶς καὶ ταχέως ἐπιστήσεται ὑμῖν,
6 ὅτι κρίσις ἀπότομος ἐν τοῖς ὑπερέχουσιν γίνεται. Ὁ γὰρ
ἐλάχιστος συγγνωστός ἐστιν ἐλέους, δυνατοὶ δὲ δυνατῶς
7 ἐτασθήσονται· οὐ γὰρ ὑποστελεῖται πρόσωπον ὁ πάντων
δεσπότης, οὐδὲ ἐντραπήσεται μέγεθος· ὅτι μικρὸν καὶ
μέγαν αὐτὸς ἐποίησεν, ὁμοίως τε προνοεῖ περὶ πάντων.
8 Τοῖς δὲ κραταιοῖς ἰσχυρὰ ἐφίσταται ἔρευνα.
9 Πρὸς ὑμᾶς οὖν, ὦ τύραννοι, οἱ λόγοι μου, ἵνα μάθητε
10 σοφίαν καὶ μὴ παραπέσητε. Οἱ γὰρ φυλάξαντες ὁσίως τὰ
11 ὅσια ὁσιωθήσονται, καὶ οἱ διδαχθέντες αὐτὰ εὑρήσουσιν
ἀπολογίαν. Ἐπιθυμήσατε οὖν τῶν λόγων μου, ποθήσατε
καὶ παιδευθήσεσθε.
12 Λαμπρὰ καὶ ἀμάραντός ἐστιν ἡ σοφία, καὶ εὐχερῶς
θεωρεῖται ὑπὸ τῶν ἀγαπώντων αὐτήν, καὶ εὑρίσκεται ὑπὸ
13 τῶν ζητούντων αὐτήν. Φθάνει τοὺς ἐπιθυμοῦντας προ-

as from a tense bow, shall they leap to the mark. From His stone-bow shall He cast hailstones full of anger; the waves of the sea shall rage against them and the rivers whelm them to the uttermost. Yea, a blast of His power shall rise up against them, and a mighty tempest shall winnow them out. So will lawlessness lay waste the whole land, and their misdeeds overturn the thrones of the mighty.

CHAPTER VI

HEAR then, ye Kings, and understand; learn, ye rulers of the ends of the earth. Give ear, ye that govern a people and glory in many nations. For dominion was vouchsafed unto you from the Lord, and sovereignty from the Most High, who will examine your works and search out your counsels. Inasmuch as, being ministers of His realm, ye judged perversely, neither guarded the Law nor walked according to the counsel of God, terribly and swiftly will He visit you, for judgement inexorable is dealt to them that have the pre-eminence. Upon the humble is bestowed mercy, but the mighty shall be mightily chastised. For the Master of All will fear no man's person, nor will He have respect unto greatness; because it is He that hath made both small and great, and considereth all alike. But upon the powerful strict inquisition cometh.

To you, therefore, O ye princes, do I speak, that ye may learn Wisdom and turn not aside. For they that have kept holy things holily will be accounted holy, and they that have received instruction will find an answer of defence. Wherefore set your affections on my words; desire them, and ye shall find knowledge.

Wisdom is radiant and unfading; readily is she beholden of all that love her, and is discovered of them that seek after her She forestalleth them that desire her, so as to be known afore

14 γνωσθῆναι. Ὁ ὀρθρίσας ἐπ᾽ αὐτὴν οὐ κοπιάσει, πάρεδρον
15 γὰρ εὑρήσει τῶν πυλῶν αὐτοῦ. Τὸ γὰρ ἐνθυμηθῆναι περὶ
αὐτῆς φρονήσεως τελειότης, καὶ ὁ ἀγρυπνήσας δι᾽ αὐτὴν
16 ταχέως ἀμέριμνος ἔσται. Ὅτι τοὺς ἀξίους αὐτῆς αὕτη
περιέρχεται ζητοῦσα, καὶ ἐν ταῖς τρίβοις φαντάζεται αὐτοῖς
17 εὐμενῶς, καὶ ἐν πάσῃ ἐπινοίᾳ ὑπαντᾷ αὐτοῖς. Ἀρχὴ γὰρ
18 αὐτῆς ἡ ἀληθεστάτη παιδείας ἐπιθυμία, φροντὶς δὲ παιδείας
19 ἀγάπη, ἀγάπη δὲ τήρησις νόμων αὐτῆς, προσοχὴ δὲ νόμων
βεβαίωσις ἀφθαρσίας, ἀφθαρσία δὲ ἐγγὺς εἶναι ποιεῖ
20 Θεοῦ. Ἐπιθυμία ἄρα σοφίας ἀνάγει ἐπὶ βασιλείαν.
21 Εἰ οὖν ἥδεσθε ἐπὶ θρόνοις καὶ σκήπτροις, τύραννοι λαῶν,
τιμήσατε σοφίαν, ἵνα εἰς τὸν αἰῶνα βασιλεύσητε.
22 Τί δέ ἐστι σοφία καὶ πῶς ἐγένετο, ἀπαγγελῶ καὶ οὐκ
ἀποκρύψω ὑμῖν μυστήρια, ἀλλὰ ἀπ᾽ ἀρχῆς γενέσεως ἐξιχ-
νιάσω, καὶ θήσω εἰς τὸ ἐμφανὲς τὴν γνῶσιν αὐτῆς, καὶ οὐ
μὴ παροδεύσω τὴν ἀλήθειαν.
23 Οὔτε μὴν φθόνῳ τετηκότι συνοδεύσω, ὅτι οὗτος οὐ
24 κοινωνήσει σοφίᾳ. Πλῆθος δὲ σοφῶν σωτηρία κόσμου, καὶ
25 βασιλεὺς φρόνιμος εὐστάθεια δήμου. Ὥστε παιδεύεσθε
τοῖς ῥήμασί μου, καὶ ὠφεληθήσεσθε.

7

Εἰμὶ μὲν κἀγὼ θνητὸς ἄνθρωπος, ἴσος ἅπασι, καὶ γηγε-
2 νοῦς ἀπόγονος πρωτοπλάστου. Καὶ ἐν κοιλίᾳ μητρὸς ἐγ-
λύφην σὰρξ δεκαμηνιαίῳ χρόνῳ, παγεὶς ἐν αἵματι ἐκ σπέρ-
3 ματος ἀνδρὸς καὶ ἡδονῆς ὕπνῳ συνελθούσης. Καὶ ἐγὼ δὲ
γενόμενος ἔσπασα τὸν κοινὸν ἀέρα, καὶ ἐπὶ τὴν ὁμοιοπαθῆ
κατέπεσον γῆν, πρώτην φωνὴν τὴν ὁμοίαν πᾶσιν ἴσα
4 κλαίων. Ἐν σπαργάνοις ἀνετράφην καὶ ἐν φροντίσιν.
5, 6 Οὐδεὶς γὰρ βασιλεὺς ἑτέραν ἔσχε γενέσεως ἀρχήν, μία δὲ

time; whoso riseth early in quest of her will not grow weary, for he will find her sitting at the gate. To meditate upon her is perfection of prudence, and he that keepeth watch because of her will be free from care, and that right soon. For Wisdom goeth about seeking such as be worthy of her; she doth manifest herself graciously unto them in their paths, and encountereth them in every thought. For the truest beginning of Wisdom is desire of discipline, and concern for discipline is love of her; and love of her is observance of her laws; and obedience to her laws is assurance of immortality, and immortality bringeth close to God. So therefore desire for Wisdom leadeth up to a kingdom.

If, then, ye delight in thrones and sceptres, ye princes of the peoples, honour Wisdom that ye may reign for ever.

What Wisdom is, and how she came into being, this shall I declare, nor hide from you her mysteries; nay, rather, I shall follow in her footsteps from the dawn of Creation, and fetch knowledge of her into the light, and shall in no wise pass the truth by.

Neither shall I take consuming jealousy as my companion, for jealousy hath no fellowship with Wisdom. Truly a multitude of the wise is salvation to the world, and a prudent King is a pillar of his people. Wherefore be instructed by my words; so shall ye be profited thereby.

CHAPTER VII

I, TOO, am mortal, as other men are, and an offspring of the earth-born Primal Man. In my mother's womb I was fashioned into flesh, in a time of ten months, being compacted in blood from a man's seed and from pleasure that came in sleep-time. At my birth I drew in the common air, and fell upon the kindred earth, and with me, as with all men, the first utterance was a cry. In swaddling-bands was I nursed with tender care. For no king had any other beginning, but for

7 πάντων εἴσοδος εἰς τὸν βίον, ἔξοδός τε ἴση. Διὰ τοῦτο
ηὐξάμην, καὶ φρόνησις ἐδόθη μοι. ἐπεκαλεσάμην, καὶ ἦλθέ
8 μοι πνεῦμα σοφίας. Προέκρινα αὐτὴν σκήπτρων καὶ θρόνων, καὶ πλοῦτον οὐδὲν ἡγησάμην ἐν συγκρίσει αὐτῆς·
9 οὐδὲ ὡμοίωσα αὐτῇ λίθον ἀτίμητον, ὅτι ὁ πᾶς χρυσὸς ἐν
ὄψει αὐτῆς ψάμμος ὀλίγη, καὶ ὡς πηλὸς λογισθήσεται
10 ἄργυρος ἐναντίον αὐτῆς. Ὑπὲρ ὑγίειαν καὶ εὐμορφίαν
ἠγάπησα αὐτήν, καὶ προειλόμην αὐτὴν ἀντὶ φωτὸς ἔχειν,
ὅτι ἀκοίμητον τὸ ἐκ ταύτης φέγγος.
11 Ἦλθε δέ μοι τὰ ἀγαθὰ ὁμοῦ πάντα μετ᾽ αὐτῆς, καὶ
12 ἀναρίθμητος πλοῦτος ἐν χερσὶν αὐτῆς. Εὐφράνθην δὲ ἐπὶ
πάντων, ὅτι αὐτῶν ἡγεῖται σοφία, ἠγνόουν δὲ αὐτὴν
13 γενέτιν εἶναι τούτων. Ἀδόλως τε ἔμαθον, ἀφθόνως τε
μεταδίδωμι, τὸν πλοῦτον αὐτῆς οὐκ ἀποκρύπτομαι.
14 Ἀνεκλιπὴς γὰρ θησαυρός ἐστιν ἀνθρώποις, ὃν οἱ χρησά-
μενοι πρὸς Θεὸν ἐστείλαντο φιλίαν διὰ τὰς ἐκ παιδείας
δωρεὰς συσταθέντες.
15 Ἐμοὶ δὲ δῴη ὁ Θεὸς εἰπεῖν κατὰ γνώμην, καὶ ἐνθυμηθῆναι ἀξίως τῶν δεδομένων, ὅτι αὐτὸς καὶ τῆς σοφίας ὁδηγός
16 ἐστι, καὶ τῶν σοφῶν διορθωτής. Ἐν γὰρ χειρὶ αὐτοῦ καὶ
ἡμεῖς καὶ οἱ λόγοι ἡμῶν, πᾶσά τε φρόνησις καὶ ἐργατειῶν
17 ἐπιστήμη. Αὐτὸς γάρ μοι ἔδωκε τῶν ὄντων γνῶσιν
ἀψευδῆ, εἰδέναι σύστασιν κόσμου καὶ ἐνέργειαν στοιχείων,
18 ἀρχὴν καὶ τέλος καὶ μεσότητα χρόνων, τροπῶν ἀλλαγὰς
19 καὶ μεταβολὰς καιρῶν, ἐνιαυτῶν κύκλους καὶ ἀστέρων
20 θέσεις· φύσεις ζῴων καὶ θυμοὺς θηρίων, πνευμάτων βίας
καὶ διαλογισμοὺς ἀνθρώπων, διαφορὰς φυτῶν καὶ δυνάμεις
21,22 ῥιζῶν· ὅσα τέ ἐστι κρυπτὰ καὶ ἐμφανῆ ἔγνων. Ἡ γὰρ
πάντων τεχνῖτις ἐδίδαξέ με σοφία.
Ἔστι γὰρ ἐν αὐτῇ πνεῦμα νοερόν, ἅγιον, μονογενές,

every man is ordained one entrance into life and one exit. So I made supplication, and understanding was given me; I called upon God and a spirit of wisdom was vouchsafed me. I chose Wisdom before sceptres and thrones, deeming wrath as nothing in comparison with her. Nor did I liken unto her any precious stone, seeing that all gold, matched with her, is but as a little sand, and silver shall be counted as clay before her. I loved her above health and beauty, and chose to possess her rather than light, because the light that issueth from Wisdom never resteth.

And with her came all goodly things together, and riches innumerable in her hands. I delighted in them, because Wisdom guideth them, notwithstanding I wist not she was their mother. As I learned her without guile, so do I share her without envy; I hide not her riches. For she is a never-failing treasure, and they that use it win friendship with God, being commended for gifts that come from discipline.

But God grant me to speak according to His will, and to think worthily of the good things given, for it is He that is the guide of Wisdom and teacher of the wise. For in His hands are both we and our words, all skill likewise and acquaintance with crafts. For He bestowed upon me sure knowledge of all that is, even to know the system of the Universe, and the force of the elements; the beginning, end, and middle of times; changes of the solstices and interchange of seasons; the cycles of years and places of the constellations; the nature of creatures and the frolics of wild beasts; power over spirits, and reasonings of men; diversities of plants and virtues of roots—yea, what things soever are secret and manifest, therein was I instructed, because Wisdom, the architect of all, was my teacher.

Now there is in Wisdom an intellectual spirit, holy, with-

28 ΣΟΦΙΑ ΣΑΛΩΜΩΝΟΣ

πολυμερές, λεπτὸν, εὐκίνητον, τρανόν, ἀμόλυντον, σαφές,
23 ἀπήμαντον, φιλάγαθον, ὀξὺ, ἀκώλυτον, εὐεργετικὸν, φιλάνθρωπον, βέβαιον, ἀσφαλὲς, ἀμέριμνον, παντοδύναμον,
πανεπίσκοπον, καὶ διὰ πάντων χωροῦν πνευμάτων νοερῶν
καθαρῶν λεπτοτάτων.
24 Πάσης γὰρ κινήσεως κινητικώτερον σοφία, διήκει δὲ καὶ
25 χωρεῖ διὰ πάντων διὰ τὴν καθαρότητα. Ἀτμὶς γάρ ἐστι
τῆς τοῦ Θεοῦ δυνάμεως, καὶ ἀπόρροια τῆς τοῦ παντο-
κράτορος δόξης εἰλικρινής· διὰ τοῦτο οὐδὲν μεμιαμμένον
26 εἰς αὐτὴν παρεμπίπτει. Ἀπαύγασμα γάρ ἐστι φωτὸς
ἀϊδίου, καὶ ἔσοπτρον ἀκηλίδωτον τῆς τοῦ Θεοῦ ἐνεργείας,
27 καὶ εἰκὼν τῆς ἀγαθότητος αὐτοῦ. Μία δὲ οὖσα πάντα
δύναται, καὶ μένουσα ἐν αὐτῇ τὰ πάντα καινίζει, καὶ κατὰ
γενεὰς εἰς ψυχὰς ὁσίας μεταβαίνουσα φίλους Θεοῦ καὶ
28 προφήτας κατασκευάζει. Οὔθὲν γὰρ ἀγαπᾷ ὁ Θεός, εἰ μὴ
29 τὸν σοφίᾳ συνοικοῦντα. Ἔστι γὰρ αὕτη εὐπρεπεστέρα
ἡλίου, καὶ ὑπὲρ πᾶσαν ἄστρων θέσιν· φωτὶ συγκρινομένη
30 εὑρίσκεται προτέρα. Τοῦτο μὲν γὰρ διαδέχεται νὺξ, σοφίας
δὲ οὐκ ἀντισχύει κακία.

8

Διατείνει δὲ ἀπὸ πέρατος εἰς πέρας εὐρώστως, καὶ
2 διοικεῖ τὰ πάντα χρηστῶς. Ταύτην ἐφίλησα καὶ ἐξεζή-
τησα ἐκ νεότητός μου, καὶ ἐζήτησα νύμφην ἀγαγέσθαι
3 ἐμαυτῷ, καὶ ἐραστὴς ἐγενόμην τοῦ κάλλους αὐτῆς. Εὐγέ-
νειαν δοξάζει συμβίωσιν Θεοῦ ἔχουσα, καὶ ὁ πάντων δεσ-
4 πότης ἠγάπησεν αὐτήν. Μύστις γάρ ἐστι τῆς τοῦ Θεοῦ
ἐπιστήμης, καὶ αἱρετὶς τῶν ἔργων αὐτοῦ.
5 Εἰ δὲ πλοῦτός ἐστιν ἐπιθυμητὸν κτῆμα ἐν βίῳ, τί σοφίας
6 πλουσιώτερον τῆς τὰ πάντα ἐργαζομένης; Εἰ δὲ φρόνησις

out fellow; manifold, subtle, easy of motion, clear in utterance, undefiled, plain, unharmed, prizing what is good, keen, unhindered, kindly, loving unto every man, steadfast, sure, void of care, all-powerful; overseeing all things, and passing through all intellectual, pure, and most ethereal spirits.

Wisdom is swifter than any motion, pervading and going through all things by reason of her purity. For she is an emanation of the power of God, and a spotless effluence of the glory of the Almighty; therefore nought that is defiled stealeth in upon her. For she is the effulgence of the everlasting light, and an unblemished mirror of the energy of God, and an image of His goodness. Though one, she can do all things; abiding in herself, she reneweth the world; and in every generation, entering into holy souls, she maketh men to be friends of God, and prophets. For God loveth nought save the man that dwelleth with Wisdom. She is fairer than the sun and high above the constellations in their order; compared with light, she is found to exceed it; for though night expelleth day, yet vice prevaileth not against Wisdom.

CHAPTER VIII

WISDOM stretcheth from one end of the world to another, with power, and ordereth all things excellently. I loved her and sought her out from my youth up; I desired her for a bride, and became enamoured of her beauty. She proclaimeth her noble birth, in that she hath fellowship with God, and the Master of all things Himself esteemed her dear. For she doth initiate into the mysteries of the knowledge of God, and chooseth out His works.

If riches are a desirable possession in life, what is richer than Wisdom who accomplisheth all things? And if prudence work-

ἐργάζεται, τίς αὐτῆς τῶν ὄντων μᾶλλόν ἐστι τεχνίτης;
7 Καὶ εἰ δικαιοσύνην ἀγαπᾷ τις, οἱ πόνοι ταύτης εἰσὶν
ἀρεταί· σωφροσύνην γὰρ καὶ φρόνησιν ἐκδιδάσκει, δικαιοσύνην καὶ ἀνδρίαν, ὧν χρησιμώτερον οὐδέν ἐστιν ἐν βίῳ
8 ἀνθρώποις. Εἰ δὲ καὶ πολυπειρίαν ποθεῖ τις, οἶδε τὰ
ἀρχαῖα καὶ τὰ μέλλοντα εἰκάζειν, ἐπίσταται στροφὰς
λόγων καὶ λύσεις αἰνιγμάτων, σημεῖα καὶ τέρατα προγι-
νώσκει καὶ ἐκβάσεις καιρῶν καὶ χρόνων.
9 Ἔκρινα τοίνυν ταύτην ἀγαγέσθαι πρὸς συμβίωσιν,
εἰδὼς ὅτι ἔσται μοι σύμβουλος ἀγαθῶν, καὶ παραίνεσις
10 φροντίδων καὶ λύπης. Ἔξω δι᾽ αὐτὴν δόξαν ἐν ὄχλοις, καὶ
11 τιμὴν παρὰ πρεσβυτέροις ὁ νέος. Ὀξὺς εὑρεθήσομαι ἐν
12 κρίσει, καὶ ἐν ὄψει δυναστῶν θαυμασθήσομαι. Σιγῶντά
με περιμενοῦσι, καὶ φθεγγομένῳ προσέξουσι, καὶ λαλοῦν-
13 τος ἐπιπλεῖον χεῖρα ἐπιθήσουσιν ἐπὶ στόμα αὐτῶν. Ἕξω
δι᾽ αὐτὴν ἀθανασίαν, καὶ μνήμην αἰώνιον τοῖς μετ᾽ ἐμὲ
14 ἀπολείψω. Διοικήσω λαούς, καὶ ἔθνη ὑποταγήσεταί μοι.
15 Φοβηθήσονταί με ἀκούσαντες τύραννοι φρικτοί, ἐν πλήθει
16 φανοῦμαι ἀγαθός, καὶ ἐν πολέμῳ ἀνδρεῖος. Εἰσελθὼν εἰς
τὸν οἶκόν μου προσαναπαύσομαι αὐτῇ· οὐ γὰρ ἔχει πικ-
ρίαν ἡ συναναστροφὴ αὐτῆς, οὐδὲ ὀδύνην ἡ συμβίωσις
αὐτῆς, ἀλλὰ εὐφροσύνην καὶ χαράν.
17 Ταῦτα λογισάμενος ἐν ἐμαυτῷ, καὶ φροντίσας ἐν καρδίᾳ
18 μου ὅτι ἐστὶν ἀθανασία ἐν συγγενείᾳ σοφίας, καὶ ἐν φιλίᾳ
αὐτῆς τέρψις ἀγαθή, καὶ ἐν πόνοις χειρῶν αὐτῆς πλοῦτος
ἀνεκλιπής, καὶ ἐν συγγυμνασίᾳ ὁμιλίας αὐτῆς φρόνησις,
καὶ εὔκλεια ἐν κοινωνίᾳ λόγων αὐτῆς, περιῄειν ζητῶν
ὅπως λάβω αὐτὴν εἰς ἐμαυτόν.
19,20 Παῖς δὲ ἤμην εὐφυής, ψυχῆς τε ἔλαχον ἀγαθῆς, μᾶλλον
21 δὲ ἀγαθὸς ὢν ἦλθον εἰς σῶμα ἀμίαντον. Γνοὺς δὲ ὅτι οὐκ

eth effectually, who is a more skilful artificer than she? And if
any man loveth righteousness, the fruits of Wisdom are virtues, for she teacheth temperance and prudence, justice and
courage, and nothing in man's life is of more value than these.
If a man withal desireth experience, she knoweth both past
and future; she is acquainted with cunning turns of eloquence
and unravelling of dark sentences; she foreknoweth signs and
wonders, and the issues of seasons and of epochs.

There I determined to be wedded unto Wisdom, knowing
that she would prove a counsellor in prosperity, a comforter
in anxiety and grief. Because of her I shall have renown among
the multitude and honour with the elders, though I be young
in years. I shall be found keen in judgement and admired in
the sight of potentates. If I be silent, they will tarry my leisure;
when I open my mouth, they will give ear; if I discourse at
length, they will lay their hand upon their lips. Because of her
I shall obtain immortal fame and bequeath an ever-during
memorial to posterity. I shall rule tribes, and nations will be
subject unto me. Dread sovereigns, when they hear of me, will
be afraid; I shall be a goodly ruler among the throng and be
valiant in war. When I come into my house, there shall I find
repose with her, for intercourse with Wisdom hath no bitter-
ness; and to live with her bringeth no pain, but pleasantness
and joy.

Now as I pondered these things and bethought me in my
heart that in kinship with Wisdom dwelleth immortality, and
that in her friendship is pure delight, and in the operations of
her hands are unfailing riches, and in communing ever with
her is prudence and a goodly report in the sharing of her
words, then I went about seeking to take her to myself.

For I was a gifted child, and obtained as my lot a virtuous
soul; nay, rather, being good, I entered an undefiled body.

ἄλλως ἔσομαι ἐγκρατής, ἐὰν μὴ ὁ Θεὸς δῷ, καὶ τοῦτο δ᾽ ἦν
φρονήσεως τὸ εἰδέναι τίνος ἡ χάρις, ἐνέτυχον τῷ Κυρίῳ, καὶ ἐδεήθην αὐτοῦ, καὶ εἶπον ἐξ ὅλης τῆς καρδίας μου.

9

Θεὲ πατέρων καὶ Κύριε τοῦ ἐλέους σου, ὁ ποιήσας τὰ
2 πάντα ἐν λόγῳ σου, καὶ τῇ σοφίᾳ σου κατεσκεύασας
ἄνθρωπον, ἵνα δεσπόζῃ τῶν ὑπὸ σοῦ γενομένων κτισμά-
3 των, καὶ διέπῃ τὸν κόσμον ἐν ὁσιότητι καὶ δικαιοσύνῃ, καὶ
4 ἐν εὐθύτητι ψυχῆς κρίσιν κρίνῃ· δός μοι τὴν τῶν σῶν
θρόνων πάρεδρον σοφίαν, καὶ μή με ἀποδοκιμάσῃς ἐκ παί-
δων σου.
5 Ὅτι ἐγὼ δοῦλος σὸς καὶ υἱὸς τῆς παιδίσκης σου, ἄνθρωπος ἀσθενὴς καὶ ὀλιγοχρόνιος καὶ ἐλάσσων ἐν συνέσει
6 κρίσεως καὶ νόμων· κἂν γάρ τις ᾖ τέλειος ἐν υἱοῖς ἀνθρώπων, τῆς ἀπὸ σοῦ σοφίας ἀπούσης, εἰς οὐδὲν λογισθή-
7 σεται. Σύ με προείλω βασιλέα λαοῦ σου, καὶ δικαστὴν υἱῶν
8 σου καὶ θυγατέρων. Εἶπας οἰκοδομῆσαι ναὸν ἐν ὄρει ἁγίῳ
σου, καὶ ἐν πόλει κατασκηνώσεώς σου θυσιαστήριον,
9 μίμημα σκηνῆς ἁγίας ἣν προητοίμασας ἀπ᾽ ἀρχῆς. Καὶ
μετὰ σοῦ ἡ σοφία ἡ εἰδυῖα τὰ ἔργα σου, καὶ παροῦσα ὅτε
ἐποίεις τὸν κόσμον, καὶ ἐπισταμένη τί ἀρεστὸν ἐν ὀφθαλμοῖς σου, καὶ τί εὐθὲς ἐν ἐντολαῖς σου.
10 Ἐξαπόστειλον αὐτὴν ἐξ ἁγίων οὐρανῶν, καὶ ἀπὸ θρόνου
δόξης σου πέμψον αὐτήν, ἵνα συμπαροῦσά μοι κοπιάσῃ,
11 καὶ γνῶ τί εὐάρεστόν ἐστι παρὰ σοί. Οἶδε γὰρ ἐκείνη
πάντα καὶ συνιεῖ, καὶ ὁδηγήσει με ἐν ταῖς πράξεσί μου
12 σωφρόνως, καὶ φυλάξει με ἐν τῇ δόξῃ αὐτῆς. Καὶ ἔσται
προσδεκτὰ τὰ ἔργα μου καὶ διακρινῶ τὸν λαόν σου δι-
καίως, καὶ ἔσομαι ἄξιος θρόνων πατρός μου.

Notwithstanding, when I perceived that I could not possess her unless God should bestow her upon me (yea, this also was a part of knowledge, to be certified whose gracious gift she was) I went unto the Lord and besought Him, and with my whole heart I said:

CHAPTER IX; XI. 23–*end*

'GOD of my fathers, and Lord of Mercy, who createdst all things by Thy word, and by Thy wisdom preparedst man to have dominion over the creatures Thou hast made, to order the world in holiness and righteousness, and to execute judgement in uprightness of heart: grant unto me Wisdom, the partner of Thy throne, and reject me not from among Thy sons.

'For I am Thy bondsman and son of Thy handmaid, a man feeble and short-lived, too young to understand judgement and laws. For albeit a man is perfect among the sons of man, yet, if he lack Thy wisdom, he shall be counted as naught. It is Thou that chose me beforehand to be King of Thy people and judge of Thy sons and daughters. Thou commandedst me to build a temple on Thy holy hill, and an altar in the city where Thou dwellest, a copy of that holy tabernacle which Thou preparedst from the beginning. With thee is Wisdom, who hath knowledge of Thy works and was there when Thou didst fashion the world; who knoweth what is well-pleasing in Thy sight, and what is right according unto Thy commandments.

'O send her forth from Thy holy heaven and from the throne of Thy glory, that, continually beside me, she may labour with me, and that I may know what is acceptable before Thee. For she knoweth and understandeth all things, and will direct me in my doings prudently, and will guard me with her glory. So shall my deeds be well-pleasing in Thine eyes, and I shall judge Thy people righteously and be worthy of my father's throne.

D

COMMENTARY

CHAPTER I

THE writer addresses the 'Judges' in the assumed character of King Solomon. Though the teaching given is applied to these Earth-rulers, it is specially aimed at the faithless Jews —mainly of the Diaspora (Dispersion). Note, in this chapter and elsewhere, that studied 'parallelism' which is characteristic of Hebrew poetry generally. Into this system rime and meter do not enter. The student is referred to Driver, *Literature of O.T.*, pp. 340 f. Cromwell may well have had this verse in mind when, after the execution of Charles I, he had a medal struck with this inscription: 'Be wise now, O ye kings, be learned, ye judges of the earth.'

1. **righteousness**: one of the most complex and difficult of the ruling ideas in O.T. Moral excellence is what is mainly intended here, but this includes the forensic meaning noticeable in much Hebrew prophecy, e.g. Amos v. 24. The magnificent words of Micah vi. 8 and the conclusion of Hosea's prophecy are typical. See Skinner's art., 'Righteousness in O.T.' in Hastings, *D.B.* St Bernard (*de Consideratione*) thus comments: 'It is a small thing to keep righteousness unless you love it as well.'

uprightness: integrity. **Simplicity**: Sirach i. 28; Enoch 91, 4. It is the reverse of double-mindedness: Lake on Acts ii. 47, Mayor on James i. 8. Cf. Eph. vi. 5; Col. iii. 22.

2. **tempt Him not**: that is, take God at His word. Note the symmetrical arrangement of these opening verses.

3. **perverse**: crooked: cf. Acts ii. 40. There is an excellent ex. in Solon's lines (quot. by Dem., *de F.L.*) 'discipline (εὐνομία) straightens out crooked judgements (δικὰς σκολιάς).'

5. The idea of discipline carries with it the notion of instruction.

4–7. See xi. 17 and Prov. ii. 9–15 with Oester ey's *nn.* The 4th v. is quoted more than once by John of Salisbury in the *Policraticus*.

soul, body: apparently the author assumes a dichotomy of human nature, whereas Paul (1 Thess. v. 23) recognizes a tripartite nature in man: see Westcott, added *n.* on Heb. iv. 12. The doctrine of tripartition (spirit=divine life-principle, soul=the personal principle wherein spirit manifests itself, body=the material organism quickened by soul) is adopted by the Alexandrian theologians, Clement and Origen. [Cf. Marc. Anton., xii. 3, Plat. Tim. 89 E, Plotinus Enn. iv. 8, 8, and the passage qu. from Sterry in Pinto's *Peter Sterry*, p. 156.]

loveth mankind: cf. vii. 23 and the beautiful words of Ps. cxlv. 9 (P.B.V.). 'Deus est mortali juvare mortalem, et haec ad aeternam gloriam via' (Pliny).

his reins: i.e. kidneys, regarded by the Hebrews as the seat of the feelings, as the heart of thought and determination: e.g. Ps. vii. 10.

holdeth the universe: viz., is its bond. The Stoic idea of the Anima Mundi: Lightf. on Col. i. 17. Cf. the opening of Ambrose's fine hymn, 'Rerum Deus tenax vigor'; Hastings, *D.B.*, vol. v, 280. Tennyson's Passing of Arthur, 'The whole round world . . . bound by gold chains about the feet of God.' The author of Wisdom challenges pantheism by representing God as a living personal Being. In a Greek inscription we find an address to Attis as 'the most High One who is the bond of the universe' (συνέχοντι τὸ πᾶν). See a notable passage in Cic., *de nat. D.* II. vii. 19.

knowledge of the voice: that is, of every human voice.

8. Justice is here personified. In Acts xxviii. 4 'Dike' is to be taken not as 'Justice' but a Goddess.

9. **Counsels of the ungodly:** Ps. i. 1. **lawless deeds:** cf. xvii. 2. Lawlessness is that state of moral license which disregards the law and is therefore of the essence of sin. Trench, *Synonyms*, s.v. ἀνομία.

10. **Ear of jealousy:** that is, God's. To ascribe to God 'jealousy' is an example of anthropomorphism characteristic of so much in O.T. What the word implies is that God vindicates His exclusive claim on all His worshippers. For other touches of anthropomorphism see iv. 18, v. 16, vii. 16.

11. **profiteth not:** it is of the nature of sin. **murmuring** (against God) **slayeth the soul:** i.e. is spiritual death.

12. Compare Prov. viii. 36, 'they that hate wisdom (or "instruction") love death.'

13. See ii. 23, 24; xi. 24. This passage is qu. in Euseb. *Prep. Ev.* 647. Man was originally righteous and immortal; he lost both his righteousness and his immortality through the Devil's envy, according to our author; according to Enoch evil was introduced by the Satans *or* his own evil act. It may

be observed that Augustine (in the *de civ. Dei*) goes so far as to say that in this passage (12–21) 'passio Christi apertissime prophetatur.'

14. **Read here the 10th chap. of the *Didache*. no poison of destruction**: this runs counter to the view that Evil is inherent in matter, as so many heathen philosophers averred but which is opposed to all Christian teaching. Observe that the personification of Death (Sheol) is probably derived from Greek mythology. See Methodius, qu. by Harnack, *Hist. of Dogma*, iii. 106 (E.T.).

16. **with Death a covenant**: Sirach xiv. 12. These words, though in a different context, occur in Isaiah xxviii. 15. Here there may be a ref. to apostate Jews indulging in pagan idolatries, specially perhaps in connexion with necromantic rites. Freewill is assured in this passage, whereas in the O.T. the doctrines of determinism and free-will are found side by side. See Maldwyn Hughes, *Ethics of Jewish Apocryphal Literature*, chap. iv. The text here is referred to in August. *Conf.* vi. 13.

lot, μερίς: Cf. ii. 9, 24; Eccles. ii. 10, iii. 22, ix. 9. **The wicked,** by their own choice, have sold themselves to the Devil, and so become his rightful property. Contrast the words of Ps. xvi. 6.

CHAPTER II

THIS chapter sets forth the creed of the thorough-going materialist. The conviction that so many of his fellow-countrymen are being led to abandon their ancestral faith, evokes the writer's stern protest. Here are the steps in the argument: (1) what is the materialist's theory? this world is all; (2) the natural sequel is hedonism (6–8); (3) this involves a sense of hatred against the godly man who shows up the ungodly (12–14); (4) but with what result? persecution of the godly in this life, but their final triumph (17–end).

1. **full of sorrow**: A.V. 'tedious.' Cf. Shakesp. *Cymb.* III. vi. 1, 'I see a man's life is a tedious one'; *K. John* III. iv. 108, 'Life is as tedious as a twice-told tale'; and Hobbes's summary of human life as 'poor, nasty, brutish, and short.'

remedy: lit. 'healing.' **from the grave**: a commonplace in literature; see the grand chapter in Job (xiv). Anacreon 43, 'dread is the depth of Hades, and grievous the descent thereto; for it is fated for him that goes down never more to return';

Simonides 39, 'in man's brief life there is sorrow upon sorrow, and death—inescapable—hangs over all alike.'

2. **at all adventure** (so A.V.): by mere chance (Eccles. ix. 11); for the phrase see Wright's *Bible Word-Book*. That the world is the result of Chance is an Epicurean doctrine. For the next words cf. Eccles. iii. 19, and the striking chapter in Marc. Aur. ii. 17.

reason but a spark: apparently a reminiscence of the Heraclitean doctrine that fire is the 'essentia' of spirit, a view adopted by the Stoics. Cf. Pope's 'Vital spark of heavenly flame.'

4. Cf. Ps. ix. 6, Eccles. i. 11 and ix. 5, James iv. 14; and below, v. 9–14. Obviously a humiliating confession.

5. **a shadow**: Soph. frag. 13 with Pearson's *n.*, Ajax 125/6, 'Behold, we are but phantoms, we that live, or fleeting shadows'; Job viii. 9; Tennyson (quoting Pindar), 'σκιᾶς ὄναρ, dream of a shadow, go.' Eccles. vi. 12. **no putting back of our end**: like the shadow on a sun-dial. **fast sealed**: that is, our destiny is fixed for ever.

6. Eccles. ii. 24. The comment of Pascal ('Of the righteous man,' in the *Pensées*) should be read.

7. Cf. Shakesp. *All's Well*, IV. v. 54–9.

8. Cf. *Lucr.* iii. 912 f., Herrick, 'Gather ye rosebuds while ye may.' Hor. *Od.* II. iii. 13–17.

10. **the poor righteous**: i.e. the Israelite who holds fast to the Law and to the Testimony.

11. 'Let us act on the principle that Might is Right' (the principle adopted by modern Dictators). Cf. the words in Hermetica, νόμος ἐκείνοις ἐστὶν ἡ ἰσχύς: Plat. *Gorg.* 484 B, where Pindar (*frag.* 152 Bowra) is discussed.

12. Cf. 20; Ps. xxxvii. 32; Pirqé Aboth (Taylor ed., 2, p. 188); Euseb. *Pr. Evang.* 678 *b*. **discipline**: the traditional unwritten law versus the Torah (Mosaic law).

14. The righteous are a standing rebuke to the godless; hence the hatred. Cf. John xv. 19.

16. **dross**: strictly 'counterfeit' (of base coin). Cf. ἀδόκιμος in I Cor. ix. 27.

18. See Matt. xxvii. 43, itself a ref. to Ps. xxii. 8–9. The passage in Plat. *Rep.* ii. 5 is familiar.

21. The denial of immortality is a sign of moral obliquity. Read the passage in Hooker, E.P. v, § 2.

22. **mysteries of God**: cf. vi. 22 (*n.*); Armitage Robinson, *n.*

on *Ephes.*, p. 235. Suffering is not necessarily punishment; it may be a token of divine love: 'whom the Lord loveth He chasteneth'; in Heb. xii. 5 (Westcott).

23. Eternity: reading ἀιδιότητος (not ἰδιότητος). Cf. the magnificent words of the Rig-Veda: 'Thou, God, whose shadow is immortality.'

24. Cf. Sirach xxv. 24 (an important place). And see Rom. v. 12, 1 Cor. xv. 21–2. Paul does not follow 'Wisdom' in accounting for the presence of death, for whereas W. attributes it directly to the Devil, Paul (like Milton) attributes it to the disobedience of Adam. The introduction, then, of sin into the world was prior to the coming of death: Clem. Rom. iii (fin.). Clem. Alex. *Strom.* vii, § 7 (Mayor). In any case death was looked on as abnormal; it did not exist originally and was never intended to be the lot of man. **envy**: alluding to the temptation of Eve, though some would refer it to Cain. The Devil, 'that old serpent,' was envious of the power and privileges of Adam; Jerome, *Epp.* cviii. 18. Cf. Thackeray, *Relation of St Paul to Jewish Thought*, pp. 50–4. Or is the allusion here to ethical rather than physical death?

For the conception of ἀφθαρσία or ἀθανασία, in place of the more general belief of bodily resurrection—which was a characteristic of post-Exilic Judaism, though this applies less to Alexandrian Jews.—Cf. W. L. Knox, *St Paul*, p. 128.

Chapter III

1. **T**HE righteous do not really die; their souls pass directly into the presence of God. No idea in this passage of a bodily resurrection; that doctrine was fully formulated later. It was assuredly taught in the Gospels and St Paul, who probably was acquainted with our book. Thackeray, *op. cit.*, p. 133.

2. **fools**: in the ethical sense; one who refuses to listen to wisdom, and sets himself against God. Cf. Ps. xiv. 1. Bacon, Essay on Atheism. **going hence**: ἔξοδος. The word came early into Christian use, and implies that death is removed to another sphere; so vii. 6; Luke ix. 31.

3. **in peace**: in well-being and safety. Not the repose of nescience. This expression passed over to the Christian inscriptions, as 'in pace.'

4. **punished**: through acts of persecution.

5. **chastened**: as part of the divine training: 1 Enoch cviii. 9; 2 Cor. iv. 17. 'Every divine probation is also, in purpose, an education' (Hort). **worthy**: Rev. iii. 4.

6. Cf. Sirach ii. 5; 4 Esdras xvi. 73; 1 Pet. i. 7. So Isocrates, *ad Dem.* § 25; Ov. *Trist.* I. v. 25, 26. For δοκιμάζω see Vaughan on Rom. i. 28. **burnt offering**: note Paul's word in 2 Tim. iv. 6 (where it signifies a *drink-offering*).

7. **visitation**: God's method of making His presence felt; 'visiting' for the purpose of safe-guarding. The word occurs also with a penal sense in many places, e.g. Ps. lix. 5; Isaiah x. 3. For other exx. of ἐπισκοπή see below 13; and iv. 15, xiv. 11, xix. 15.

shine: they shall not only live but be glorified for ever: Dan. xii. 3, 1 Enoch civ. 2, Matt. xiii. 43.

stubble: Obad. 18. Cf. Shakesp. *Coriol.* II. i. 274–5. The sense is: in the Judgement, the righteous, like a blazing fire, will destroy the godless.

8. In purely pictorial terms Jesus promises His disciples that they shall sit on twelve thrones, judging the tribes of Israel. Cf. Dan. vii. 22, 'judgement was given [in the Messianic kingdom] to the saints,' i.e. faithful Israel. Specially noteworthy is the parallel passage in 1 Cor. vi. 2. The **ungodly** in next v. are renegade Jews.

10. **the righteous man**: perhaps τοῦ δικαίου here is neut.= Justice, as in Col. iv. 1.

11. **faith** (or 'hope'), ἐλπίς. Only here. It implies acceptance of the divine will, and perfect trust in this. For the opening words cf. Prov. i. 7.

12. **children evil**: Sirach xli. 5. A characteristic piece of Jewish belief, which is certainly not always borne out by experience.

13. **conceived in sin**: that is, by marriages contracted with heathen. **fruit**=reward.

14. The Deuteronomic law attached a religious stigma to eunuchs. Here the godly eunuch is found acceptable. **more desirable**: viz. than the pleasures of wedded life.

18. **no hope**: of leaving posterity.

19. The theory was that sin is punished even in this life: cf. iv. 3–4. The belief, set forth in this chapter, that the children of the godless are penalized for their father's sins, is controverted by Jeremiah xxxi. 29–30. See R. H. Kennett, *O.T. Essays*, chap. 2; S. A. Cook, *Laws of Moses and Hammurabi*,

p. 261. Readers of the Gospels will remember how this grave matter was dealt with by Jesus Himself in the memorable 9th chap. of John.

CHAPTER IV

1. **virtue**: in the usual sense of moral excellence. In classical Greek ἀρετή has no necessary ethical significance; it denotes any kind of excellence. Hort on 1 Pet. ii. 9; Mayor on 2 Pet. i. 3.

2. **take example thereat**=imitate it. The next clause suggests the well-known words of Hor. *Odes*, III. xxiv. 31; Pers. iii. 38. Cf. Milton, *P.L.* iv. 847–9. **walketh in triumph**: like a Roman general, crowned with the laurel-wreath of victory, marching up to the Capitol. **rewards undefiled**: the prize of immortality. The word ἀμίαντος occurs three times in N.T. in its metaph. meaning.

5. **branches broken**: see the parallel in Sirach xxiii. 25. **inquisition**: at the Judgement Day.

7. **at rest**: as in iii. 3. For ἀνάπαυσις cf. Sirach vi. 28, where it signifies tranquillity of mind. Here rather=a state of (or 'place of') rest.

8, 9. Aptly quoted by John of Salisbury, *Policraticus*, 562. Cf. Prov. xvi. 31 (R.V. marg.); Sirach xxv. 4–6. Similar are the words found in the laws of Manu (to which Strabo refers): 'the hoar head is not revered by the gods unless it be accompanied with wisdom and knowledge (τὸ φρονεῖν); such a man, though young, is old.'

10. Here Enoch is alluded to: Moffatt on Heb. xi. 5. Sirach (xliv. 16) follows another tradition than that shared by the author of Hebrews. The author of Wisdom holds that God removed Enoch that he might not fall into (further) sin. But cf. Cyprian, *de immort*. xvi.

12. Such are the subtle enticements of sin that it darkens the moral sense (τὰ καλά), being apt to turn even a guileless man giddy, through the whirl of passion. Jeremy Taylor, *Holy Living*, ii. § 1.

13. **perfected**: brought to glory as the consummation of bliss.

brief season: Enoch's life was short by comparison with that of Methuselah (and others). It is the quality of life that matters, not its duration.

15. The resemblance here to 1 Enoch i. 8 is not to be missed. **visitation**: of mercy, in this connexion.

18. **in derision**: Ps. ii. 4; Prov. i. 26. **hereafter, etc.**: at the day of decision. Compare the dramatic passage in Isaiah iv, where Sheol (personified) mocks at the entrance of the Babylonian King to the grim underworld.

19. **in anguish**: there is no hope, then, of annihilation for the ungodly; they suffer in Gehenna.

speechless: conscience is too much for excuses; Matt. xxii. 12.

memorial, etc.: they will be completely forgotten: cf. Job xviii. 17; Ps. ix. 6; Psalms of Solomon xiii. 10, 'sinners will be carried away to destruction, and the memorial of them shall no more be found.' Apostate Jews are indicated.

20. St Paul's words in Romans ii. 5–9 are appropriate here.

CHAPTER V

1. **confidence**: in Greek, the primary meaning is 'boldness of speech'; cf. Abbott on Eph. iii. 12. The wicked, on the other hand, will be speechless: iv. 19.

2. Observe 'the revulsion of feeling on the part of the wicked when confronted with the victims of their abuse' (Fairweather). So 1 Enoch cviii. 15, 'sinners shall cry aloud when they behold the righteous in glory.'

3. **repenting**: not in the nobler sense, but 'with remorse.' See Trench, *Syn*. § 69.

4. **madness**: because they (the godly) refused earthly gains if the price of such gains involved unfaithfulness to the Law.

5. Quoted by John of Salisbury, *Policr*. 493 *d*.

7. **highway**: obedience to the Law. Note that the 'Way' is an early name in N.T. for the Church: Lake on Acts ix. 2.

9 f. A vivid series of pictures to denote the transitoriness of life; cf. ii. 15; Shakesp. *Macb*. v. 3, 'Life's but a walking shadow'; P.-B., Prayer for the Church militant, 'this transitory life.' **rumour** (or 'messenger'; A.V. 'post'): Wright, *Bible Word-book*.

11. May we call to mind the unforgettable simile in Bede (*Eccl. Hist*. ii) of the bird flying through a lighted hall, and out again into the darkness?

14. **foam**: but for ἄχνη there is a variant reading ἀράχνη, a spider's web. **remembrance of a guest**: memoria hospitis

unius diei praetereuntis; Pascal *Pensées* (on Man's dispro-
portion).

15. Cf. ii. 23. Most High, ὕψιστος: only twice in this book; see
vi. 3. Often in Sirach, as a title of God; so in Luke (several
exx.); generally in N.T. only in passages which have an O.T.
ring, or in sayings attributed to the possessed: Swete on Mark
v. 7.

16. **His right hand,** etc.: cf. Ps. cxviii. 16; Pss. of Solomon,
xiii. i, 'the right hand of the Lord overshadoweth me.'

17 f. For the 'panoply of God' see the great Pauline passages in Eph. vi. 10–17, 1 Thess. v. 8, both based on Isaiah
lix. 17.

jealousy, ζῆλος: viz. intense and holy zeal. We have no one
apt word to render it. Cf. John ii. 17.

21 f. Jehovah stirs up the powers of Nature to fight against
the godless. Similarly in Sirach xxxix. 29. The wrath of God
(i.e. His moral indignation against sin) is an essential element
in His holiness. It must not be explained away. Cf. John iii.
36; Eph. v. 6. Lactantius, in his treatise *de ira Dei*, shows, in
contrast with the Epicureans, that the divine character is
capable of righteous anger, and that our conception of that
character would be imperfect unless we included this attribute. As Bevan justly says: 'the idea that God cannot be
angry is a Pagan, not a Christian idea.' Hooker, in *Eccl. P.*
VI. v. § 1, quotes from Basil, Augustine, and Cyprian; see San-
day and Headlam on Rom. i. 18; Orr in Hastings, *D.B.*, vol. i,
s.v. ANGER. Perhaps we may affirm that the divine wrath re-
acts automatically on the sinner, whereas His mercy—inherent in the very nature of God—issues not as a response to
human endeavour but as something freely bestowed.

stone-bow, Lat. *ballista*: an engine used in sieges for hurling
ponderous stones: Rich, *Dict.* Cf. 1 Macc. vi. 51.

CHAPTER VI

IN this chapter Solomon, the assumed writer of this book,
gives his kingly counsel to the world's autocrats.

3. Rom. xiii. 1, 'the powers that be are ordained of God,'
i.e. authority is delegated to them. This indeed is orthodox
Jewish doctrine; cf. 1 Enoch xlvi. 5; Dan. iv. 25. But when the
principle is involved in Jewish literature it is usually, as here,
as a menace to those who misuse their authority (as Dodd

has observed). Paul draws a different inference; all authority
is declared to be of divine origin: so 1 Pet. ii. 13.

4. **ministers**: as ultimately responsible to God. Cf. the
words of Justin M., lxviii, 'you will not escape if you persist in
acting unjustly'; John of S., *Policr.* 455 *a*.

5. **have the pre-eminence**: the Greek word occurs in 1
Pet. ii. 13; Rom. xiii. 1.

7. **no man's person**: God, being strictly impartial, has no
favourites: Deut. xi. 17; Acts x. 34; James ii. 1 (with Mayor's
n.); Pss. of Sol. ii. 19, 'God is a righteous Judge and is no respecter of persons.' John of S., *op. cit.* 532 *c*, 554 *a*.

8. **inquisition**: ἔρευνα, lit. 'a strict inquiry.' In those days
such an inquiry, in the secular courts, was often made by tor-
ture.

10. **defence**: when summoned to give account of their
stewardship.

12. Infr. vii. 28–9; Prov. iii. 15–17. For **unfading** = ἀμάραντος,
cf. 1 Pet. i. 4, where it is combined with ἀμίαντος and ἄφθαρτος.
The word, says Hort, exhibits in a figure the essential sense of
αἰώνιος, the negation of mutability and perishableness.

14. Read the memorable words of Deut. xxx. 11–14.

15. **prudence**, φρόνησις: almost equiv. to 'commonsense'
here. For a discussion of this word in Greek philosophy, see
Grant on Aristot., *Eth.* vi. 5, and for the distinction between
it and σοφία Abbott on Eph. i. 8.

15. Elsewhere in the *Ethics* Aristotle says (VI. xiii. 6), 'the
single virtue of practical wisdom (φρόνησις) involves all the
virtues.' There is a fine passage in a letter of Epicurus to his
friend Menoeceus (quoted by Diog. Laert. x. 132): 'The supreme good is prudence; it is more precious than philosophy;
from it spring all the virtues, for it teaches that we cannot
lead a life of pleasure which is not also a life of prudence,
honour, and justice; nor lead a life of prudence, honour and
justice which is not also a life of pleasure.'

17. **discipline**, παιδεία: once more this point is stressed; cf.
i. 5; Sirach iv. 17. The reader will note the use of what is
called 'sorites' (chain-inference) here. The *O.E.D.* defines it
thus: 'a series of propositions in which the predicate of each is
the subject of the next, the conclusion being formed of the
first subject and the last predicate.'

18, 19. See Euseb. *Eccl. Hist.* v. viii. 8, who quotes the
saying of Irenaeus: 'the vision of God bringeth incorruption.'

True it is also that the vision of God is the call of the Prophet, now as ever. The study of the Law, says a Jewish Targum, is a sure principle of immortality.

20. **a kingdom**: in a spiritual sphere.

22. **mysteries** (cf. ii. 22): in the sense of spiritual truths, once unknown but now revealed, as distinct from merely 'esoteric' doctrines, such as we meet with in Oriental cults, to be interpreted only to Initiates by the hierophant. There is nothing of this in the Gospels, which courts publicity (see Wernle, *Beg. of Christianity*, ii. 124). It has been pointed out by Holmes that the Alexandrian Jews had syncretized their religion with Greek speculations, but, unlike the heathen who jealously guarded their secrets, were eager to propagate their synthetic creed. See Angus, *The Mystery Religions and Christianity*, pp. 18 f., 187 f. The cult of Serapis was a triumph for this 'theocrasia,' as it is termed. For the word μυστήριον see Abbott on Eph. i. 9, Lightfoot on Col. i. 26.

23. **fellowship with wisdom**: Vaughan on Rom. xii. 13 for the word κοινωνεῖν. 1 John i. 3, 'we (Christians) have fellowship with the Father. Greek thinkers are prone to stress the misery entailed by envy (φθόνος); as one of them beautifully says, 'Envy stands outside the divine choir' (Plato, *Phaedrus*, 247).

24. 'Unless,' says Plato (*Republic*, 473), 'philosophers win kingly power in states, or kings be imbued with genuine philosophy, there will be no deliverance for cities nor for mankind.'

CHAPTER VII

SOLOMON is introduced as speaking to encourage his hearers.

1. **Primal Man**: Adam, אדם. The Greek word (πρωτόπλαστος) taken over by English writers, e.g. Glanvill and Browning, in form 'protoplast,' occurs again (x. 1) and is frequently found in Patristic writings. Harnack, *Hist. of Dogma*, vol. iii, 106 (E.T.); 1 Cor. xv. 47.

2. **ten months**: lunar months=280 days, the normal period of gestation.

3. **common air**: so Isocrates speaks of a ἱερὸν κοινόν, a temple open to all; Juvenal xv. 148, communis conditor mundi (of God). **fell upon**: it was customary in antiquity to set a newborn babe on the ground immediately after birth. **a cry**: Lucr. v. 226, 'the baby, like a sailor cast away by the waves,

lies naked on the ground; he fills the room with rueful cries'
(see Munro's *n*.); Shakesp. *K. Lear*, IV. vi. 182; G. Herbert, 'I
wept when I was born and every day shows why.' There is a
good parallel in [Plato] *Axiochus*, 366, and again in Pliny,
N.H. vii. 2. 'Man alone, at birth, cast naked on the naked
earth, is abandoned to cries and lamentations.' Burton, *Anat.
of Mel.* I. ii. 3 (10).

7. Quoted by Ruskin, *Fors*, Letter 60. Cf. chap. ix and the
beautiful opening of 2 Chronicles i. 7 f. (the dream of Solomon).

8, 9. Job xxviii. 12–18; Prov. viii. 10–11. The next verses
are quoted several times in the Policraticus.

10. light: cf. 29. Yet 'truly the light is sweet' (Eccl. xi. 7).

12, 13. I wist not, when first I prayed for wisdom. share,
or 'communicate.'

14. Cf. viii. 18. friendship with God: so in 27. In James ii.
23 Abraham is called God's friend; cf. John xv. 15. Plato,
Rep. 612, 'the righteous man is θεοφιλής'; *Laws*, 716, 'the wise
man is a friend of God, for he is like Him'; Xen. *Memor.* II. i.
33 [Virtue is speaking in the Allegory of Prodicus] 'through
me men become friends of God'; Book of Jubilees, xix. 9
(Abraham) 'was found faithful and enrolled on the heavenly
tablets as the friend of God.' Cf. Scott on *Hermetica*, vol. iii.
298. gifts: or perhaps, 'graces'—the result of discipline, or
moral training.

16, 17. Compare Hooker, *Eccl. P.* I. vii. 7. Knowledge of
all that is, viz. philosophy. Like Bacon, Solomon would annex
all knowledge as his province. The King would have wel-
comed the great dictum of the philosopher when he wrote
'the sovereignty of man lieth hid in knowledge' (*The praise
of Knowledge*, 1592). Universe, κόσμος. This meaning of the
word is fully established in the Apocrypha. And so throughout the N.T., e.g. John i. 10; Acts xvii. 24; Rom. i. 20. elements. στοχεῖα, i.e. earth, air, fire, water. A term familiar in
Greek philosophy, but well known to the Hellenized Jews of
Alexandria. For the list in the next two verses see a similar
passage in [Plato] *Axiochus*, 370.

20. Zoology, meteorology, psychology, botany and medi-
cine, astronomy. In 1 Kings iv. 33, we are given a list of some
of Solomon's reputed accomplishments. A host of legends
gathered about him in Oriental countries: see, e.g. Sirach
xlvii. 13-18. reasonings of men, viz. Logic.

22. See Oesterley on Proverbs viii. 30. **Architect** (τεχνῖτις), not creator but artificer, master-craftsman. Cf. 2 Cor. ii. 6–16. Paul's language on the influence of the Spirit has points of resemblance with what is said about σοφία, wisdom, here. Cudworth's words are parallel: 'Νοῦς (Mind) is senior to the world and the Architect thereof.' It may be noted that the whole section 17–22 is quoted in full by Eusebius in *Prep. Evang.* xi. 7.

23. **subtle** (so A.V.) or 'ethereal': that is, purely immaterial. Shakespeare's *Tempest*, Ariel, *'fine apparition.'* For the accompanying list of 21 epithets in 22–3 see *added note*.

24 f. The terms used here are technical in Greek metaphysics. In v. 26 Wisdom is described after the manner of a Greek philosopher discoursing on Νοῦς, the universal Mind. As sharing in God's throne (ix. 4) Wisdom stands for supreme power, justice, providence, mercy; in fact all the divine attributes meet in Wisdom. It is difficult to be certain whether Wisdom, is, in itself, a poetic personification or a divine personality, separate from though subordinate to God. Wisdom is certainly presented as co-operant with God in creation, but we cannot indeed affirm that our author actually identifies it with the Absolute One. The treatment of the subject is not too clearly defined; it wavers.

power, ἐνέργεια=power in operation. The word occurs eight times in N.T. For the Aristotelian view of this important word consult the essay in Grant's *Ethics of A.* vol. i. It is, to use Calvin's definition, 'potentia in actu exserens,' the activity whereby potential power (δύναμις) is exhibited.

25. **emanation**: literally, 'vapour' (ἀτμίς). The word put into the mouth of Wisdom in Sirach xxiv. 3 is ὀμίχλη.

effluence (ἀπόρροια): cf. the Jewish conception of the Shekinah, or Manifestation of Deity (Taylor, Pirqe Aboth, iii, *n.* 8). The word is not in O.T. Origen writes on this verse with his usual discursiveness in the *de Principiis,* i.

27. A favourite text with Augustine, who quotes it four times in the *Confessions;* see also *de fide et symbolo,* § 3. For the thought of the unchangeable nature of God, see the following: Job. xxiii. 13; Mal. iii. 6; Heb. vi. 17; James i. 17.

abiding in herself: unvarying and unchanged in nature. Heb. i. 10–12; Pope's *Essay on Man,* i. 267–80.

reneweth: Ps. civ. 30; Isaiah xliii. 18–19. The thought is akin to that of 2 Cor. v. 17. Cf. Rev. xxi. 5. Creation is no single act, but a continuous process.

28. **dwelleth with**, as with a bride. The conception of a divine marriage, though strange to us, is imbedded in O.T. teaching: cf. Hosea ii. 19–21; Isaiah liv. 6. The imagery taken over by the writers of the Gospels, to reappear in a heightened form in the Apocalypse (xix. 7, xxi. 9). See S. H. Hooke in *The Labyrinth*, chap. vi.

Additional Note on 22, 23

Here we have a list of twenty-one epithets applied to Wisdom (7×3: symbolic numbers). Probably the writer was not influenced in his choice of words by strictly philosophical considerations: rhetoric plays its part. There is a list of wisdom epithets, eight in number, in James iii. 17: only one of these appears in our list. Somewhat in like fashion epithets of the Supreme Being are heaped together in the Upanishads, without much regard to order, and sometimes even contradictory. In the list here printed the English equivalent of each Greek word is taken from the R.V. and put within inverted commas.

(1) 'quick of understanding,' intellectual; νοερός, a technical word of the Stoics, and frequent in the Hermetica.

(2) 'holy': ἅγιος is rare in Attic Greek; it does not, apparently, occur in Homer, Hesiod, or in the Tragedians. The fundamental notion of the word is separation (from sin), with the concomitant idea of consecration (to God). Here, as in two N.T. passages, the word may connote *requiring holiness* in others.

(3) 'alone in kind': μονογενής, sui generis; Lat. unicus. It occurs several times in Lxx. For its use in Christian theology see Hort, *Two Dissertations*.

(4) 'manifold': πολυμερής as distinct from μονογενής. In Heb. i. 1 we find the adv. πολυμερῶς.

(5) 'subtil': λεπτός. Cf. Eur. *Med.* 1081. In N.T. only as neut. noun=a farthing.

(6) 'freely moving': εὐκίνητος, *mobile*. So ὀξυκίνητος is used, in Philo, of the Logos.

(7) 'clear in utterance': τρανός (late form of τρανής). See Gataker on Antoninus, ix. § 30. Or=penetrative.

(8) 'unpolluted': ἀμόλυντος; see under καθαρός (21).

E

(9) 'distinct': σαφής. Or=perspicuous; therefore a sure guide. The word, though common, is not in N.T.

(10) 'unharmed', i.e. not subject to injury. But it may be active: wisdom *inflicts* no injury.

(11) 'loving what is good': φιλάγαθος; Titus i. 8.

(12) 'keen': ὀξύς, with a cutting edge. Cf. Heb. iv. 12, where the divine Logos is pictured as a living active thing, sharper than a two-edged sword.

(13) 'unhindered': ἀκώλυτος. Or=irresistible. The adv. occurs at the end of Acts.

(14) 'beneficent': εὐεργετικός, as in Aristot. *Rhet.* II. xi. 4.

(15) 'loving towards man': φιλάνθρωπος, as in i. 6. The Vulg. gives humanus, benignus (two words for one in Greek).

(16) 'steadfast' (or=unchangeable): βέβαιος.

(17) 'sure': ἀσφαλής. Or=unfaltering, unfailing. The moral signification is less common than the social and political.

(18) 'free from care': ἀμέριμνος; Matt. xxviii. 14; I Cor. vii. 32. It implies freedom from worldly distractions. Could it have an active sense here—care-dispelling?

(19) 'all-powerful': παντοδύναμος. Observe the use of παντοκ ράτωρ in the Creeds: Swete on Rev. i. 8. [It may perhaps be worth noting that in a Christian prayer (Grenfell and Hunt, Oxyr. Pap. vi. 291) God is addressed as παντοκράτωρ. Frequent in Lxx. and ten times in N.T.]

(20) 'all-surveying': παντεπίσκοπος. Cf. Clem. Alex. *Strom.* 837 (the worldly and disillusioned) 'deny the existence of God, or declare that, if He exists, He is not the overseer of all.' Prov. xv. 3 (with Malan's *nn.*).

(21) 'pure': καθαρός, viz. clear of pollution or shame. Cf. James i. 27 (where ἀμίαντος=ἀμόλυντος) and iii. 17 (where ἅγιος is used instead of καθαρός).

CHAPTER VIII

1. The diffusion of wisdom throughout the world. **ordereth** (διοικεῖ): another Stoic term. In the life of Zeno by Diog. Laert (vii, § 133) one of the questions put forward by Zeno's school was 'whether the Universe is ordered by Providence (προνοία).' 'An ordered Universe,' urged Marcus Aurelius (iv. 27); 'otherwise a welter of confusion. Assuredly, then, a world-order.' See the Collect for 8th Sunday after Trinity.

excellently: or 'graciously.'

2–18. The discourse of Virtue in the famous story of the Choice of Heracles should be carefully compared with these verses (Xen. *Memor*. ii. i. 32 f.).

2. Prov. vii. 4, 'Say unto Wisdom, thou art my sister.' **lover,** ἐραστής: one of the many Platonizing words in the book. Cf. Plato, *Symp*. 204, 'Wisdom is a most beautiful thing, and Love is of the beautiful, and therefore a lover of wisdom.'

3. **fellowship,** συμβίωσις: cf. 9, 16 and vii. 28 (*n*.). Philo calls God the husband of Wisdom. **proclaimeth,** i.e. acknowledges the glory of.

4. **mysteries of the knowledge:** vi. 22 (*n*.). The phrase 'knowledge of God' occurs nearly a dozen times in O.T. and N.T., e.g. Prov. ii. 5; Hosea vi. 6; Rom. xi. 33. Such a knowledge is no abstract theory, no mere intellectual assent, but implies an intimate acquaintance with a Person.

chooseth out, as an active agent in creation.

6. **prudence,** φρόνησις, is set over against true wisdom, σοφία, as the earthly compared to the divine. Cf. *n*. on vi. 15.

7. The four Cardinal[1] Virtues (as 'primary') are given here as in 4 Macc. i. 18. They were taken over from Plato by the Stoics; cf. Plat., *Rep*. 428, 433; *Laws*, 631; Cic. *de Off*. i. v, 15 f.; *Diog. Laert*. vii. 92. This passage of Wisdom is quoted by Clem. Alex. *Strom*. 787; see, too, 838 (=vii, § 17). Cf. Mackenzie, *Manual of Ethics*, pp. 340 f.; Rabelais, *Pantagruel*, iii. ii; W. R. Sorley, *The Moral Life*; Bernard, *de Consolatione*, i. vii.

temperance: self-control. This virtue holds a most important position in Greek philosophy (σωφροσύνη). See a definition in Plat. *Symp*. 196; *Gorg*. 507 (Thompson); *Rep*. 430; Prof. A. E. Taylor's *Plato*, pp. 47 f., 249. For N.T., Trench, *Synonyms*. More at length in Aristot. *Eth*. iii. 10. In 4 Macc. i. 31 the definition given is quite in the Platonic vein.

8. **past and future:** one thinks of the impressive words in Isaiah xlvi. 9–10. **turns of eloquence:** Sirach xxxix. 2–3. **unravelling:** solving riddles or expounding allegories. Prov. i. 6; Sirach xlvii. 17. **signs and wonders:** eclipses. The combination of these two words occurs often in N.T. but with a different meaning. **issues,** viz. crises in human history.

9. All through this next section the writer is speaking in the person of the young King, Solomon.

12. **hand upon their lips:** Job xxi. 5; Micah vii. 16.

---

[1] The word 'Cardinal' is of Christian origin; it is apparently first found in Ambrose: Sidgwick *Hist. of Ethics*, p. 133.

16. Wisdom will secure domestic peace as well as success in statecraft.

17. The wise of heart share with Wisdom her own immortality.

18. Cf. vii. 14.

19. **gifted:** A.V. 'witty,' a word which, like 'cunning' and 'crafty' has suffered degeneration: Wright, *Bible Word-book*. The word in Greek is εὐφυής, thus explained by Aristotle in the *Ethics*, III. v. 17: 'he is truly a man of parts (or quick of intellect) who has the inborn power of discriminating aright and choosing the good.' See Cope on Arist., *Rhet.* I. vi. 15.

20. **undefiled body:** the pre-existence of *soul* (נֶפֶשׁ, nephesh) is probably indicated; see the close of 4 Maccabees, and Oesterley, *Immortality*, p. 18. The 'virtuous soul' is the personality, the thinking self, to which God allots a body: cf. Maldwyn Hughes, *Ethics of Jewish Apocr. Lit.*, 177–80. The writer of Wisdom is acquainted with the Platonic view; the source is not in O.T. That the Jews of our Lord's time had some inkling of the doctrine of the soul's pre-existence may be conceded: John ix. 2, 'Who sinned—this man (i.e. in a former life) or his parents that he was born blind?' In later Judaism the theory was common enough. It should be noticed that, in our passage, the body is not regarded as irredeemably evil; souls are good or bad when they enter upon a bodily existence: see Charles, Secrets of Enoch, xxiii. 5. It has been observed that Roman Catholics who deny the doctrine of pre-existence, necessarily boggle over 19, 20, because the Tridentine Fathers affirmed that 'Wisdom' was a part of the canonical Scriptures, and therefore inspired. Ref. may be made here to Aquinas, *Summa c. Gentiles*, §§ 83, 84; for Indian speculations see Monier-Williams, *Indian Wisdom*. That Origen taught this doctrine is obvious to any reader of the *de Principiis*; the resolute opposition to it in the Church was on account of its connexion with Oriental and Greek speculation.

Note that the second half of v. 20 serves as a correction to what has preceded.

21. **possess her:** Sirach vi. 27, 'take hold of Wisdom, and let her not go.'

CHAPTER IX

1. **Lord of mercy:** Hosea vi. 6 (a text twice quoted by Jesus) 2 Cor. i. 3. Mercy is essentially the divine attribute, as Shakespeare saw: *M. of V.* IV. i. 203.

all things by Thy word (word and wisdom being here equated): Sirach xlii. 15. This is perhaps the germinal idea of the Logos doctrine, but is not identical with the 'logos' of the Johannine prologue. See a note in Scott's *Hermetica*, vol. iii, p. 51.

2. holiness and righteousness: as in the 'Benedictus.' A familiar combination. Cf. Eph. iv. 24. For the distinction between holiness (towards God) and righteousness, or justice (towards man) see Trench, *Synonyms of N.T.* This verse indicates that God's purpose in creation is always the *Good*. Cf. Dean Matthews's *The Purpose of God*.

4. partner of Thy throne: Prov. viii. 27, 30. Cowper's hymn, 'Hark, my soul.' A fine parallel in [Demosthenes] xxv. § 11, 'Remember you are under the eyes of inexorable and sacred Justice, who sits by the throne of the high God and surveys all the works of men.' Other classical refs. are, Pind. *Ol.* viii. 21; Soph. *O.C.* 1382.

5. too young: 1 Kings iii. 7.

8. temple: 2 Sam. vii. 13. The 'holy hill' is Mount Moriah. Ps. xlviii. 1. A copy: Exod. xxv. 40. Remark the use made of the O.T. passage in Heb. viii. 5 (with Moffatt's *n.*). Similarly in Plato where the *Idea* is regarded as the eternal pattern of all things in nature; this is alluded to in Milton, *P.L.* v. 575. Not that the author of 'Wisdom' must necessarily have had recourse to Plato for his notion of the heavenly archetype, as this is not unfamiliar in Semitic writings. In later Jewish theology there was a heavenly as well as an earthly Jerusalem. And see the closing chapters of the Apocalypse.

9. with Thee is wisdom: cf. Prov. viii. 22 f., where Wisdom is depicted as present at the Creation.

11. with (or 'in') her glory: the brightness shed by Wisdom on her disciples.

13. A ref. to Isaiah xl. 13, 14. Cf. 1 Cor. ii. 11. The verse is quoted by John of S., *Policrat.* 584 *a*. Read Montaigne's discussion in his *Essays*, ii. 12.

14. timorous (A.V. 'miserable'), that is, vacillating. Sirach ii. 12 f. For thoughts, λογισμοί, cf. Romans ii. 15.

15. This very important v. is quoted by Augustine in the *Confessions*, vii. 15. The metaphor of a tent (σκῆνος) for a human body is a phrase which finds its counterpart in the Pauline epistles, 'the earthly house of our tabernacle (tent) in which we groan' (2 Cor. v. 1–4), but is nearer to Orphism than to Jewish thought. That the body is a prison for the soul—

E2

σῶμα, σῆμα—was common among Pythagorean philosophers, and the notion was adopted by Plato as we see by referring to the *Phaedo*, 81 and the pseudo-Platonic *Axiochus*, 365–6. It appears to have been fundamental in Alexandrian thought, and was later taken up by Origen: see his *de Principiis*, ii. 10. In the *Hermetica*, xiii. 15, we read, 'you are purified, having put off the tent.' Cf. Romans vii. 24; 2 Pet. i. 13; Ep. to Diognetus, 6; and Field's *n.* on the Corinthians passage in his *Otium Norvicense* (Did St Paul there lean towards the doctrine of the inherent evil of matter?). Latin writers touch upon all this, e.g. Virg. *Aen.* vi. 730–4; Cic., *de Senect.* xxi. Certain aphoristic words in the Laws of Manu might be cited: see Monier-Williams, *Indian Wisdom*, p. 283. We find Wordsworth too, writing of the 'shades of the prison-house' in his great Ode. Reference may be made to Adam, *Religious Teachers of Greece*, p. 385. Add Hor. 2 *Sat.* ii. 77; Spenser, Sonnet 72.

16. 'We walk by faith, not by sight,' says St Paul. Cf. John iii. 12; 2 Esdras iv. 21.

17. The parallelism here has led some to think that Wisdom is identified with the Holy Spirit of God; but surely not in the later Christian sense? Cf. here 1 Cor. ii. 11, 16. There is, however, no certainty that Paul borrowed directly from our author, though he may very probably have been influenced indirectly by Alexandrian philosophy.

18. How **saved**? by turning the hearts of the disobedient to the wisdom of the just. The remaining chapters of this book are a commentary on this truth.

CHAPTER XI. 23–*end*

23. Compare the opening of the Collect for 11th Sunday after Trinity. **overlookest**: see Acts xvii. 30. Punishment is primarily remedial; Rom. ii. 4. Later on in the book of Wisdom (xv. 1–2) we find a similar notion; and Paul may well have had that passage in mind.

25. So in Clem. Alex. *Strom.* vii. § 69, 'God is creator of all things, and there is no existing thing that He does not love.' Cf. Collect for Ash Wednesday.

26. **lover of souls** (or 'lives'): cf. i. 13; Ezek. xxxiii. 11.
abideth: the Anima Mundi; cf. on i. 7.

SELECT GLOSSARY

ἀγαθότης, *goodness*; i. 1, vii. 26. Sirach xlv. 23. Rare (not in N.T.); commoner form ἀγαθοσύνη. Exx. in ancient homily attributed to Clem. Rom. xiii; Philo, Plato theologus; Clem. Alex., e.g. *Strom.* 795, ἀγαθὴ ἡ τοῦ Θεοῦ δικαιοσύνη καὶ δικαία ἡ ἀγαθότης.

ἀγγελία, *message*; v. 9. So generally in Lxx. In 1 John iii. 11= commandment. See L. and S.

ἀγερωχία, *arrogance*; ii. 9. Cf. 2 Macc. ix. 7.

ἀθετέω, *despise, reject*. Several times in Lxx. Cf. 1 Tim. v. 12; 1 Macc. xv. 27.

ἀϊδιότης, *eternity*; ii. 23. [There is an alternative reading ἰδιότητος (for ἀϊδιότητος)=peculiar nature, proper being.] The adj. ἀΐδιος occurs twice in N.T., Rom. i. 20, Jude 6.—See Inge, *Plotinus*, vol. ii, 92.

αἴνιγμα, *dark saying*, viii. 8; as in Sirach, xxxix. 3; xlvii. 15. Blomf. Gloss on *Agam.* 1081.

αἱρετίς, *chooser* (Vulg. 'electrix'); *lover* A.V.; viii. 4.

ἀλαζονεία, *boasting*; v. 8. Only twice in N.T. Mayor on James iv. 16. Cf. Theoph. *Char.* vi (Jebb).

ἀνεκλιπής, *unfailing*; vii. 14, viii. 18 (=endless).

ἀνομία, *lawlessness*; v. 7, 23. A state of moral license; Rom. vi. 19.

ἀνωφελής, *unprofitable*; i. 11. In this sense some five times in Lxx. Cf. Psalms of Sol. xvi. 8. Twice in N.T.

ἀπαύγασμα, *effulgence*; vii. 26. A characteristic Alexandrian word. Cf. Westcott on Heb. i. 3; Clem. Rom. xxxvi, who quoted the passage in Hebrews.

ἀπόρροια, *effluence*; vii. 25. Cf. Marc. Aur. ii. 4, v. 27, ἀπόσπασμα θεοῦ; Hermetica, 'another shall come to dwell among men, an efflux of My being (τῆς ἐμῆς ἀπορροία φύσεως).' Diog. Laert. viii. 28.

ἀπιστέω, *distrust*; i. 2. The verb and its noun ἀπιστία not in Lxx, and ἄπιστος only in Isa. xvii. 10. ἀφθαρσία, *incorruption, immortality*; ii. 23, vi. 19, 20. Lightf. on Ignatius, vol. ii, p. 73, and p. 276, 'the Gospel is the coping-stone of immortality.' Often in O.T.—See Armitage Robinson on Eph. vi. 24.

βασίλειον, *Kingdom, palace*; i. 14. Ryle and James on Ps. of Sol. xvii. 7. So in Lxx. Cf. Wetstein on Luke vii. 25.

βασκανία, *witchery*; iv. 12. For the verb cf. Sirach xiv. 8. Metaphor from the popular belief in the Evil Eye: Lightf. on

Gal. iii. 1. See text discovered in 1899 on a papyrus roll: Milligan, *Greek papyri*, 55, l. 9.

γαυρόω, in mid: *make one's boast in*; vi. 2. Cf. Numbers xxiii. 24, 3 Macc. iii. 11.

διάβολος, *the devil*; ii. 24. Swete on Rev. xii. 9. By this word the Lxx renders the Hebrew שׂטן.

εἰλικρινής, unsullied; vii. 25. Mayor on 2 Pet. iii. 1.

ἔκβασις, *ending, close*; ii. 17. Heb. xiii. 7. But *infr.* viii. 8 in a different sense.

ἐπιείκεια, *gentleness*; ii. 19, xii. 18. So in 2 Macc. ii. 22. Mayor on James iii. 17; Lightf., Phil. iv. 5. For its use in Greek philosophy, Aristot. *Eth.* v. 10. Matthew Arnold's 'sweet reasonableness.'

ἐπισκοπή, *visitation*; iii. 7, 13; iv. 15; xiv. 11; xix. 15. Ps. of Sol. iii. 14; Hort on 1 Pet. ii. 12. May be used in good or bad sense: cf. Sirach ii. 14 and xviii. 20.

εὐστάθεια, *stability, steadfastness*; vi. 24. Ps. of Sol. vi. 7; 2 Macc. xiv. 6.

εὐφυής, *goodly* or *gifted*; viii. 19. It implies a good natural disposition, of mind or body or both: Cope on Aristot. *Rhet.* 1. vi. 15.

κινητικός, *mobile*; vii. 24.

μεταλλεύω prop. means 'dig mines'; iv. 12. 'The A.V. here adroitly covers by a happy analogy what appears to be a simple mistake,' translating the word by 'undermines.' The writer is confusing μεταλλεύω with μεταλλοιόω.

μονογενής: see vii. 22. In N.T. we translate by 'only begotten' as applied to Christ, but 'only' in Luke vii. 12, etc. Here= *alone of its kind* (sui generis), as in Plato, *Timaeus*, εἷς οὐρανὸς ὅδε μονογενὴς ὤν (92; cf. 31). In Clem. Rom. xxv. of the phoenix. For other exx. of this interesting word see Ps. xxii. 23, xxxv. 17; Judges xi. 34; Tobit iii. 15, viii. 17.

μυστήριον, *mystery*; ii. 22. Cf. Abbott on Eph. i. 9; Hatch, *Essays in Biblical Greek*. [In xiv. 15 of heathen rites.]

μύστις, *initiated* (if used as adj.); viii. 4.

ὁμοιοπαθής, of like qualities=*kindred*; vii. 3.

ὁσιότης (ix. 3) is hard to define. Grote renders it 'holiness,' Jowett 'piety.' Cf. Mayor, Cic. *de nat. D.* 1. § 116.

παιδεία, *disciplinary instruction*; i. 5. Cf. Eph. vi. 4; 2 Tim. iii. 16.

πειράζω, *test*; iii. 5. The noun πειρασμός in Sirach ii. 1, and often in N.T.

πετροβόλος, Lat. 'ballista'; v. 22. Polybius, Josephus, and elsewhere.

πολύφροντις, *much-musing* (multa cogitans); ix. 15. Rare and poetical.

πρωτόπλαστος, *first-formed*; vii. 1 (cf. x. 1). Exx. in Eus. *Pr. Ev.* 549, Clem. Alex. 559, etc., and (in Latin) Tertullian, Cyprian, Prudentius.

ῥεμβασμός, *whirling* (noun); iv. 12.

σκολιός, *crooked, perverse*; i. 3. Acts ii. 40; Phil. ii. 15 (=Deut. xxxii. 5).

στοιχεῖον, in plural=*elements*; vii. 17. Cf. xiii. 2, 3 (i.e. heathen deities). Thackeray, *Relation of St Paul to Jewish Thought*, 163–70; Burton's discussion in his ed. of Galatians, 510–18. The word is regularly used of the four elements from Aristotle onward.

στροφή, *turn*; viii. 8, where the pl. signifies 'eloquent turns of oratory' as in Aesch. *Suppl.* 623. Cf. στρέφειν λόγους in Plat. *Gorg.* 511.

συγγνωστός, *pardonable*; vi. 6 ('exiguo conceditur misericordia').

σύγκρισις, *comparison*; vii. 8. The verb occurs in v. 29.

συμβίωσις, *companionship*; viii. 3, 9, 16. Sirach xxxi. 22; Cic. *ad Att.* xiii. 23.

συναναστροφή, *intercourse*; viii. 16. So in Eus. *Pr. Ev.* 375; 3 Macc. ii. 33.

σωφροσύνη, *sobriety* (of behaviour), *self-control*; viii. 7. See Jowett's Introduction to the Charmides. 2 Macc. iv. 37.

ὑποστέλλω, *shrink from, fear* (in midd.); vi. 7. Cf. Deut. i. 17.

φιλάνθρωπος, *loving unto men*; i. 6; vii. 23; xii. 19. Connected with ἐπιεικής in 2 Macc. ix. 27 (adverbs). Cf. Murray, *Five Stages*, 156, 158 (Thinker's Library ed.). There is an interesting note on the word in Aristotle, *Poetics*, 1452 (Bywater). Cf. φιλανθρωπία in N.T., Titus iii. 4.